Geo. S. Morris.

HEINE'S

BOOK OF SONGS.

HEINE'S

BOOK OF SONGS.

TRANSLATED BY

CHARLES G. LELAND,

AUTHOR OF "MEISTER KARL'S SKETCH-BOOK" AND "SUNSHINE IN THOUGHT."

PHILADELPHIA:
FREDERICK LEYPOLDT.
NEW YORK: F. W. CHRISTERN.
1864.

Entered, according to Act of Congress, in the year 1863, by

FREDERICK LEYPOLDT,

In the Clerk's Office of the District Court of the United States
for the Eastern District of Pennsylvania.

ELECTROTYPED BY L. JOHNSON & CO.
PHILADELPHIA.

Das ist der alte Mährchenwald.

'TIS the old wood of fairy tales!
The linden scent steals round me;
And the wild, lovely moonlight ray
With fairy charm has bound me.

And on I went, and as I went,
Above I heard a ringing;
And all of love and loving pain
Dame Nightingale was singing.

She sings of love and pains of love,
Of tears and laughs out-breaking;
She chirps so sad, she sighs so glad,
Forgotten dreams awaking.

And on I went, and as I went,
I saw before me lying,
In a broad field, a castle fair,
Quaint gabled, upward flying.

Enclosèd windows everywhere,
  A silence full of warning;
It seemed as though the peace of Death
  Dwelt here in awful mourning.

Before the doorway crouched a sphynx,
  Dread, with love longing human;
The claws and body lion-like,
  In head and breasts a woman.

A lovely one, whose rising glance
  Showed Love to Passion turning;
The silent lips were bent to kiss,
  Smiling assent—and burning!

So sweetly sang the nightingale,
  I yielded as a lover;
And as I kissed the lovely face,
  With me 'twas quickly over.

All living grew the marble form,
  Blood through each vein flushed burning;
The flaming glow of my kisses hot
  She drank with thirst and yearning.

She well-nigh drank my breath away,
  And then, in lust up-flaring,
Twined round me, all my wretched limbs
  With lion-talons tearing.

Ravishing death! voluptuous pangs!
  Infinite pain and pleasure!
The talons tore with agony,
  While I sucked the mouth's rich treasure.

Sang nightingale: "O lovely Sphynx,
O Love! what is the reason
That you still bring death's keenest pain
To love's most rapturous season?

O lovely Sphynx! O riddle wild!
In vain I still revolve it:'
I've turned it many a thousand year,
But never yet could solve it."

—ALL of that I could have very well said in good prose. . . . But when one reads over his old poems in order to retouch them a little for a new impression, the jingling *habit* of rhyme and metre steals over him unawares, and, lo! it is with verses that I begin the third edition. O Phœbus Apollo! if these verses are bad, you will kindly pardon me. . . . For you are an omniscient god, and well know why I have not since many years busied myself much with metre and harmony. . . . You know why the flame which once delighted the world with brilliant flashes of fire-works must all at once be suddenly applied to far more serious conflagrations. . . . You know why it now in silent glow consumes my heart. . . . You understand me, great, beautiful god, since you too have now and then exchanged the golden lyre with the strong bow and the deadly arrows. . . . Do you not remember Marsyas, whom you flayed? That was long ago; and there is need of a fresh example. You smile, O my immortal father!

Written in Paris, February 20, 1839.

HEINRICH HEINE.

CONTENTS.

Dream-Pictures.

PAGE
I had a dream long since of Love's wild glow........................ 1
A dream right strange, yet dread to see 2
I saw myself—'twas in a dream by night................................ 5
In dreams I saw a little dandy fellow.................................... 5
What headlong madness stirs my blood?................................ 6
In sweetest dreams by silent night 8
I have paid you your price, but you're lingering still............ 10
I went from the house of my lady fair.................................. 14
I lay and slept, and softly slept.. 20
I've called the pale dead round me...................................... 21

Songs.

When night flies, I ask the morrow...................................... 23
Now here, now there I'm urged—at last................................ 23
All under the trees I wandered.. 24
Love, my love,—lay your small hand on my heart................. 25
Lovely cradle of my sorrow.. 25
Wait, oh, wait, impatient sailor 26
Hills and towers are gazing downward.................................. 27
I at first was near despairing... 28
With roses, with cypress, and gold-leaf bright...................... 28

Romances.

PAGE
THE MOURNER.—Every tender heart shows feeling.................. 30
THE MOUNTAIN ECHO.—A rider through the valley passed....... 31
TWO BROTHERS.—On yon mountain-summit dreaming............. 31
POOR PETER.—1. Jack and his Maggie go dancing around....... 33
" " 2. Deep in my breast's a pain alway.................. 33
" " 3. Poor Peter wanders, tottering, by................ 34
SONG OF THE PRISONER.—Folks said, when my granny Eliza bewitched.. 35
THE GRENADIERS.—To the land of France went two grenadiers.. 35
THE MESSAGE.—Now rise, my squire, and saddle quick........... 37
TAKING HOME THE BRIDE.—I go not alone, my dainty love...... 38
DON RAMIRO.—Donna Clara! Donna Clara!............................ 38
BELSHAZZAR.—Midnight came slowly sweeping on................. 44
THE MINNESINGERS.—To the strife of song forth wending....... 46
LOOKING FROM THE WINDOW.—Pale Henry caught fair Hedwig's eye.. 47
THE WOUNDED KNIGHT.—I know a mournful reading............. 47
THE VOYAGE.—I counted every falling wave.......................... 48
THE BALLAD OF RUE.—Sir Ulrich in the green wood rides....... 49
TO A LADY SINGER.—Even now, as when I first beheld her.... 51
SONG OF THE DUCATS.—O my golden ducats! say................... 52
DIALOGUE ON THE PADERBORN HEATH.—Hear'st thou not far music ringing.. 53
LIFE-GREETING.—This earth of ours is a great highway.......... 55
YES, INDEED.—When spring is coming with sun-rays bright... 56

Sonnets.

TO A. W. VON SCHLEGEL.—In wide-hooped dress and flowers of gaudy brightness.. 57
TO MY MOTHER, B. HEINE, NÉE VON GELDERN.
1. It is my wont my head right high to carry.... 58
2. In wild delusion from thy side once turning 58
TO H. S.—I oped thy book in haste, and, lo, before me.......... 59

Fresco Sonnets to Christian S.

PAGE

I dance not with, I worship not, that rabble........................ 60
Give me that mask,—for masked I'll cross the border........... 60
Loudly I laugh at the dry, soulless flunkey........................... 61
My brain is haunted by a legend rare.................................. 61
When the soft evening hours are sadly going........................ 62
When I saw thee again in last year's meeting....................... 63
Beware, my friend, of devilish grins and glaring.................. 63
Thou'st seen me oft with knaves in altercation...................... 64
I would be weeping, yet I cannot weep................................ 65

Lyrical Intermezzo.

1822—1823.

PROLOGUE.—There once was a knight, sad and silent was he... 66
In the wondrous lovely month of May................................. 68
Up from my tears are growing 68
For the dove or the sun, rose or lily sweet growing............... 68
Whene'er into thine eyes I see... 69
That face which ever fair did seem.................................... 69
Oh, lay thy cheek against my cheek................................... 70
I will pour all my soul's deep feeling.................................. 70
The stars have stood unmoving... 70
On the wings of song far sweeping.................................... 71
The lotus-blossom suffers 72
In the Rhine, in the glorious river..................................... 73
You love me not, you love me not...................................... 73
Come, twine in wild rapture round me................................ 74
Oh, do not vow, but only kiss 74
Upon my darling's lovely eyes... 75
The world's a fool, the world is blind.................................. 75
Dreamy phantoms, fair and fleeting 75
Like the foam-born of the waters 76
I *will* be patient, though my heart should break 77
Yes, thou art wretched, but I'll not complain........................ 77
Viol and flute are sounding 78
So you have forgotten altogether.. 78
And if the small flowers but knew it................................... 78

PAGE
Why are the roses so pale of hue.. 79
O'er me they much lamented.. 80
The lindens blossomed, the nightingale sung........................ 80
We've had many a sympathetic thought............................. 81
To me thou wert true the longest..................................... 81
Too long had the earth kept back its treasure..................... 82
And as I so long, oh, so long delayed................................ 83
O'er violets blue her eyelids fall.. 83
The world is so fair, and the heaven so blue....................... 83
My own dear love, when in the tomb................................. 84
A pine-tree's standing lonely.. 85
Lovely, gleaming, golden star... 85
Ah! could I but the footstool be.. 86
Since my sweetheart went away 86
From the great pain of my spirit....................................... 87
Too oft I cannot bless thee... 87
Town-snobbies, their Sunday keeping................................ 88
The forms of times forgotten.. 88
A young man loves a maiden.. 89
The Elixir Vitæ, friendship, love 90
Hear I the ballad ringing 90
I dreamed of the fairest princess seen............................... 91
My love, in our light boat riding....................................... 91
From ancient legends springing 92
I have loved thee long, and I love thee now........................ 93
On a fair gleaming summer morning 93
In the dark garb she's wearing.. 94
They tortured me completely.. 94
The ruddy rays of summer.. 95
Often when two are parting.. 96
With feelings refined and poetic.. 96
My songs are full of poison... 97
The dream of old came o'er me 98
I stand upon a mountain 98
My coach goes slowly rolling.. 99
I wept while I was dreaming.. 100
Each night in dreams thou com'st to me 100
The wind and the rain are playing 101
The Fall wind rattles the branches..................................... 101
Yonder a star is falling.. 102

PAGE

The Dream-God brought me to a giant pile 103
The midnight air was cold and rude 104
The suicide lies buried 104
Where I am, still darker o'er me 105
Night lay upon my eyelids 105
The old and evil ballads 107

The Homeward Journey.

1823—1824.

In my life too dark and dreary 109
I know not what sorrow is o'er me 110
My heart, my heart is weary 111
In the woods I wander weeping 112
The night is wet and stormy 112
As I once by chance on a journey 113
We sat by the fisher's cottage 114
My gentle ferry-maiden 115
The moon is high in heaven 116
The quiet moon upon the clouds 116
All wrapped up in gray cloud-garments 117
The wild wind puts his trousers on 118
The wind pipes up for dancing 118
The night comes stealing o'er me 119
When early in the morning 120
The ocean shimmered far around 121
High up on yonder mountain 122
Far on the dim horizon 123
Once more in solemn ditty 123
Again through the streets well known of old 124
I entered her home, recalling 125
Calm is the night, and the city is sleeping 125
How canst thou sleep so calmly 126
The maiden sleeps in her chamber 126
I stood in shadowy dreaming 127
I, a most wretched Atlas, who a world 128
Ages may come and vanish 128
It seemed that the pale moon sadly shone 128
What means this lonely tear-drop 129
The pale half-moon is floating 130

PAGE
To-night we have dreadful weather 131
They say that my heart is breaking 132
Oh, thy lovely lily-fingers 132
Has she really never noticed 133
They tenderly loved, and yet neither 133
When first my afflictions you heard me rehearse 134
I called the Devil, and he came 134
Mortal! sneer not at the Devil 135
Which is the way to Bethlehem 135
My child, we once were children 136
My heart is sad, and with misgiving 137
As the summer moon shines rising 138
In dreams I saw the loved one 138
Friend of mine, why are you ever 139
But, I pray, be not impatient 140
It is time that my mind from this folly I free 140
The great King *Wiswa-mitra* 141
Heart, my heart, oh, be not shaken 141
Thou'rt like a lovely floweret 142
Child! it were your utter ruin 142
When on my bed I'm lying 143
Maiden with thy mouth of roses 143
Though, without, the snow-drifts tower 144
Many pray to the Madonna 144
And do not my pale cheeks betray 144
Dearest friend, you are in love 145
I fain would linger near thee 145
Bright sapphires are your beaming eyes 146
With love-vows I long have bound me 147
This world and this life are so scattered, they try me 147
To-night they give a party 148
I would I could blend my sorrows 148
Thou hast diamonds, and dresses, and jewels 149
He who for the first time loves 149
No! the tameness and the sameness 150
They gave me advice which I scarcely heeded 150
I can never speak too highly 151
I dreamed that I was Lord of all 152
From sweetest lips have I been forced, and driven 154
We rode in the dark post-carriage 154

PAGE

Lord knows where the wild young hussy..... 155
When you become my married wife..... 156
Like dusky dreams, the houses..... 156
What lies are hid in kisses..... 157
Upon your snowy bosom..... 158
Blue hussars with their trumpets loud sounding..... 158
I too, in life's early season..... 159
Seldom did we know each other..... 159
How the eunuchs were complaining..... 159
'Twas just in the midst of July that I left you..... 160
Near to me lives Don Henriquez..... 160
Round the walls of Salamanca..... 161
Now then, do you really hate me?..... 162
Still the same those eyes beguiling..... 162
Scarce had we met, when, in tones and in glances..... 163
The sunlight is stealing o'er mountain and river..... 163
On strange roads the night is lying..... 164
In the market-place of Halle..... 164
Summer eve with day is striving..... 165
Death is a cool and pleasant night..... 165
Say, where is your own fair darling..... 166
THE TWILIGHT OF THE GODS.—The month of May with golden gleams is coming..... 166
RATCLIFF.—The Dream-God brought me to a rural scene..... 169
DONNA CLARA.—In the pleasant twilight garden..... 173
ALMANZOR.—1. In Cordova's grand cathedral..... 176
2. Hastily from the cathedral..... 178
3. In the castle Alcolea..... 180
THE PILGRIMAGE TO KEVLAAR.
1. The mother stood at the window..... 181
2. The Virgin Mary at Kevlaar..... 182
3. The sickly son and his mother..... 183

The Hartz Journey.

1824.

PROLOGUE.—Black dress-coats and silken stockings..... 185
MOUNTAIN IDYLS.—1. On yon rock the hut is standing..... 186
" " —2. Fir-tree with his dark-green fingers..... 188
" " 3. Silently the moon goes hiding..... 190

PAGE
THE SHEPHERD BOY.—Every shepherd is a monarch................ 194
THE BROCKEN.—In the East 'tis ever brighter........................ 195
THE ILSE.—I am the Princess Ilse... 196

The North Sea.

1825–1826.

PART FIRST.

HOMAGE.—Ye poems! ye mine own valiant poems!................ 198
TWILIGHT.—On the white strand of Ocean............................. 200
SUNSET.—The sun in crimsoned glory falls........................... 201
NIGHT ON THE SEA-SHORE.—Starless and cold is the night..... 203
POSEIDON.—The sun's bright rays were playing..................... 205
DECLARATION.—Onward dimly came the evening................... 207
BY NIGHT IN THE CABIN.—The sea has many pearl-drops....... 209
STORM.—Loud rages the storm... 212
CALM AT SEA.—Ocean silence! rays are falling...................... 213
A SEA-PHANTOM.—But I still leaned o'er the side of the vessel 214
PURIFICATION.—Stay thou in gloomy ocean-caverns............... 217
PEACE.—High in heaven the sun was standing...................... 218

PART SECOND.

SEA-GREETING.—Thalatta! Thalatta!................................... 220
STORM.—Dark broods a storm on the ocean........................... 222
THE SHIPWRECKED.—Lost hope and lost love! All is in ruins.. 223
SUNSET.—The beautiful sun-orb.. 225
THE SONG OF THE OCEANIDES.—Colder the twilight falls on the Ocean.. 227
THE GODS OF GREECE.—Thou full-blooming moon! in thy soft light.. 230
QUESTIONING.—By the sea, by the dreary, darkening sea........ 233
THE PHŒNIX.—A bird from the far west his way came winging 234
ECHO.—I leaned on the mast; on the lofty ship's deck.......... 235
IN PORT.—Happy the man who is safe in his haven............... 236
EPILOGUE.—As in the meadow the wheat is growing.............. 239

I.

Mir träumte einst von wildem Liebesglühn.

I HAD a dream long since of Love's wild glow—
Locks, mignonette and myrtle—all it teaches
Of sweet red kisses and of bitter speeches;
Sad airs of sadder songs—long, long ago!

My soaring dreams long since their wings have folded
And passed away, so too that visioned form;
All that remains is what in passion's storm
Once in rapt love in my soft rhymes I moulded.

Thou, orphaned song, art here! go seek the wraith
Of that sweet dream so long from me retreating,
And when thou find'st it, give my truest greeting:
I send to the airy shade an airy breath.

II.

Ein Traum, gar seltsam schauerlich.

A DREAM right strange, yet dread to see,
Delighted once yet frightened me:
E'en yet I see its grisly forms,
E'en yet my heart still heaves with storms.

There rose a garden very fair,
And I was glad to wander there;
There looked upon me pleasant flowers,
They gave me hope of golden hours.

There birds were chirping in the grove
Full many a charming song of love;
The red sun shot a golden ray
On all the flowers in colors gay.

Sweet perfumes stole among the trees,
And light and loving blew the breeze,
And all was gleaming, all was glad,
And all for me in splendor clad.

And in this lovely flower-land
I saw a marble fountain stand;
And washing linen in the stream
I saw a maiden in my dream.

Sweet cheeks, mild eyes, with glances faint,
The blonde-haired picture of a saint;
And as I looked, the maid seemed grown
So strange, and yet of old well known.

And as she urged her task along,
The maiden sung an elvish song:
"Water, water, run and shine!
Wash my linen fair and fine!"

Then slowly to her side I drew,
And said, "O maiden, tell me true,
Fair as the fairies, sweet and bright,
For whom is washed this garment white?"

"Be ready soon!" she said aloud,
"It is for you I wash the shroud;"
And scarce her words were spoken through,
When forth like foam the vision flew.

And yet enchanted still I stood,
Deep in a dark and gloomy wood;
The trees to heaven their branches raised,
And I stood thinking, all amazed.

And hark! a heavy echo rose,
As though some axe struck distant blows.
In haste through brake and bush I roam,
And then into a clearing come.

And central in the verdant space
A mighty oak had found a place;
And see! the maiden strange and fair
Was hewing with a hatchet there!

Blow fell on blow; between each stroke,
She sang her song to axe and oak:
"Iron mine, iron shine!
Cut the oaken coffer fine!"

Then slowly to her side I drew,
And said, "I pray you, tell me true,
Young maiden strange, and wondrous fair,
For whom is meant the coffer there?"

"Short time is left," she quickly spoke,
"I cut your coffin from this oak;"
And scarce her words were spoken through,
When forth like foam the vision flew.

All dead and pale around me lay
A barren heath, far, far away;
I could not tell how came the thing,
Or how I came there shuddering.

And as I wandered on my way,
A brighter place before me lay.
I hastened still, I hastened more,
And found the form I saw before.

On wide-spread heath stood blonde-white maid,
And dug the earth with burial spade;
I hardly dared to look, for she
Was fair yet fearful still to me.

And as she urged her task along,
The maiden sang an elvish song:
"Spade, my spade, sharp and tried,
Dig the grave out deep and wide!"

Then slowly to her side I drew,
And said, "I pray you, tell me true,
Young maiden strange, and fair, and sweet,
What means this grave before our feet?"

And quick she spoke, "Be still! it's true—
This cool, deep grave I've dug for you;"
And as the lovely maid replied,
The grave before me opened wide.

And as the opening grave I view,
A freezing horror thrills me through,
And plunging in its funeral might
I fall—but wake once more to light.

III.

Im nächt'gen Traum hab' ich mich selbst geschaut.

I SAW myself—'twas in a dream by night,
A black dress-coat and silken waistcoat showing,
With ruffled hands as to a party going,
And by me stood the loved one, fair and bright,
And with a bow I said, "The bride!—ah—right!
Accept my compliments,"—but the glib flowing
Of words was checked; my very throat seemed growing
To stop this flippant, cold, and well-bred rite;
When all at once I saw that she was weeping
Such a wild flood of tears, swelling with sighing,
That her dear form seemed well-nigh from me sweeping.
O gentle eyes; dear love-stars fondly gleaming,
Although awake, I oft have seen ye lying.
I trust ye still,—aye, though ye lie while dreaming.

IV.

Im Traum sah ich ein Männchen klein und putzig.

IN dreams I saw a little dandy fellow,
Who walked on stilts, each step a yard or two;

He wore white linen and a garment new,
But all within was coarse, and foul, and yellow;
Yes, *all* within was mean, corrupt, and mellow,
Although he seemed *without* both sound and true.
And much the creature bragged of courage, too;
And saucy was his strut, and loud his bellow.

"And know you *who* that is? Come here and see!"
So spoke the Dream-God, slyly showing me
Dim pictures in a magic glass, and then
Before an altar stood my dwarf in dress,
My loved one near him, and as both said, "Yes!"
A thousand devils, laughing, cried, "Amen!"

V.

Was treibt und tobt mein tolles Blut?

WHAT headlong madness stirs my blood?
What drives my heart with fiery goad?
My blood boils up, ferments, and foams,
And o'er my heart grim anger comes.

My blood boils up, and mad I seem,
For I have had an evil dream;
There came the gloomy Son of Night,
Who bore me, gasping, in his flight.

He took me to a lighted house,
Mid sound of harp and gay carouse;
Mid tapers' gleam and torches' glare,
I reached the hall and entered there.

It was a merry marriage-feast,
Gay at the table sat each guest;
But when the bridal pair I spied,
Oh, woe! my darling was the bride!

It was my love, but in my room
A stranger stood, and he the groom!
Behind the bride's own stately chair
Silent I stood, still waiting there.

Sweet music sounded,—still I stood,
Gay sounds awoke my mournful mood;
In every glance the bride seemed blest,
The bridegroom oft her fingers prest.

The bridegroom filled his beaker high,
And drained it deep, then courteously
Gave to the bride; she smiled to thank:—
Oh, woe! my crimson blood she drank!

A dainty apple then she took,
And gave it him with loving look;
Across the fruit his knife he drew,—
It was my heart he cut in two.

They glance so sweet, they glance so long,
He dares embrace, nor deems it wrong;
Her red lips feel his kisses free,—
But, oh! cold Death is kissing me.

My tongue lay in my mouth like lead,
No single word could I have said;
The music rolled, the dance began,
The dainty bride-pair led the van.

While I stood corpse-like on the ground,
The dancers swept so wild around;
The groom speaks whispering to the bride :—
She blushes,—but she does not chide!

* * * * *

VI.

Im süßen Traum bei stiller Nacht.

IN sweetest dreams by silent night
There came to me, through magic might,
The one whom I love best of all,
She came into my chamber small.

I gazed upon the lovely child,
I gazed on her, she softly smiled,—
Smiled till my wildest love awoke,
And boldly, madly, thus I spoke:

"Take all, take what thou wilt of me,
What most I love I'll give to thee,
If thou wilt be my paramour
From midnight to the dawning hour."

She looked on me mysteriously,
So sweetly, sadly, earnestly,
Then said, in all her loveliness,
"Give thy eternal happiness!"

"My life so sweet, the life of youth,
I'd give with joy in very truth:
To thee, thou angel, both are given,
But ask not for my hopes of heaven."

Quickly the daring word was said,
But fairer, fairer seemed the maid,
Still whispering in her loveliness,
"Give thy eternal happiness!"

Harsh on my ear the answer fell;
There rolled the burning sea of hell
To the last recess of my soul;
Scarcely a breath could I control.

White angels o'er me pinions spread,
With golden glories round each head;
But storming wildly, at their back,
Came grisly swarms of goblins black.

They battled with the angels white,
They drove away the angels white;
But then I saw the black array
In cloudy vapor fade away.

Oh, then I burned to taste her charms,
And held my darling in my arms;
She twined around me like a roe,
But wept, and all in bitter woe.

She weeps; the cause I know full well,
And kiss her little rose-lips still.
"O sweetheart, cease this flood of tears,
Yield to my love, and not to fears!

"Yield to my love."—Scarce spoke I twice,
When at one shock my blood seemed ice;
Deep groaned the earth, then opened fleet
A black abyss before my feet.

And from the black abyss, like hail,
Shot the dark fiends; my love grew pale!
Far from my arms my love has flown,
But I am left, and all alone.

Then in a ring and all around
The devils dance with maddening bound,
And close they press, and on me spring,
While screaming yells of mockery ring.

And closer grows the ring around,
And madder roars the shuddering sound,
"Thou gav'st away salvation free,
Thou'rt ours to all eternity!"

VII.

Nun hast du das Kaufgeld, nun zögerst du doch?

I HAVE paid you your price, but you're lingering still,
With your brow dark as blood,—knave,—go do as I will!
In silence alone in my chamber I bide,
And midnight is coming,—I wait for the bride.

There's a shuddering breeze from the burying-ground:
"O breeze! do you know where my bride may be found?"
Pale spectres take figures aerial and thin,
And murmur, "Oh, yes!" with strange greeting and grin.

"Unpack now!—and give me your message entire,
You swarthy-faced scoundrel in livery of fire!"
Their graces the company quickly approach:
They soon will be here in their state-dragon-coach.

"Little gray mannikin, what do you seek?
Long-buried schoolmaster, what is it?—speak!"
Sadly he looks, but has nothing to say,
And, shaking his head, he goes tottering away.

What a shaggy scamp, with his wag and bark!
What a devilish glare from the cat in the dark!
What a howl from those women with waving hair,
While my old nurse is singing my cradle-song there!

"Good nurse, your dull sing-song will tire me at last,
The time for a lullaby's long ago past;
To-day is my wedding; to-day is a feast,—
Just look! and see coming each elegant guest!

"Just look, now! That's stylish, I vow, and well-bred;
For a hat, every gentleman carries his head!
You spindle-legged folks in your gallows-array,
No wind has been blowing to keep you away!"

Old witch-mother Broomstick comes sweeping anon:
"Come bless me now, Motherkin, I am your son!"
With the trembling lips of a sorceress dread,
"Amen to eternity!" Motherkin said.

Twelve wind-dried musicians come hobbling in;
Blind Fiddle-wife stumbles along between.
Jack Pudding comes jigging with Harlequin Jack,
Bearing the grave-digger in pick-a-back.

Twelve nuns from a cloister come dancing this way,
And a squinting old pander-wife leads the array;
Twelve lusty young friars come close pressing on,
Singing sinful songs in a clerical tone.

"Old clothesman, why yell till your face is dead
blue?
In hell-fire that fur cloak no service can do!
There they heat it gratis year in, year out,
With the bones of prince or of beggar-lout."

Crooked-backed flower-girls, tumbling to ground,
Go stumbling their somersaults everywhere round.
"Grasshopper-legs with the face of an owl,
Cease rattling your ribs, and be still with your howl!"

All hell together is loose, I see,
Raving and waving in myriads free;
While the waltz of damnation begins to hum :—
Hush! hush!—for my darling the bride is come!

"You rabble, be silent, or get you all gone!
I scarcely can hear any word of my own,—
And there comes the sound of a carriage and four!
Hey, Cook!—oh, where are you?—run, open the
door!"

"Oh, welcome, my darling. And how is my dear?
Your Reverence is welcome,—there's place for you
here!
Your Reverence with horse-hoof and wonderful tail,
I am yours to command, sir,—nor fear I shall fail."

"My bride, my beloved!—why pale and so still?
The priest and the wedding but wait for your will:
As dear as heart's blood is his horrible fee,
But it seems a mere toy, since it gives you to me.

"Kneel down by me, darling, my beautiful bride!"
She kneels, she is sinking—oh, joy!—at my side:
She sinks on my heart, on my wild-beating breast,
And with shuddering rapture her charms are caressed.

Her wild hair in gold waves hides us both in its play,
On *my* heart the maid's heart is beating away,
And throbbing with agony, burning with bliss,
We soar to a region more raptured than this.

Our hearts in an ocean of ecstasy swim
In regions celestial and holy to HIM,
But still on our heads, as a curse and a brand,
All hell to eternity presses its hand.

And the priest in his robes is the dark Son of Night,
Who gives us the blessing which quenches our light;
From a blood-written volume he murmurs each verse,
The prayer is black blasphemy, blessing is curse.

There is crashing and hissing to madden the soul,
Like the roaring ocean or thunder-roll;—
A blue flame flashes above our head,—
"Amen to eternity!" Motherkin said.

VIII.

Ich kam von meiner Herrin Haus.

I WENT from the house of my lady fair,
I wandered in madness and dark despair;
And as by the churchyard I went my way,
Sadly the gravestones signed me to stay.

The minstrel's tombstone made me a sign,
In the glimmering light of the pale moon's shine:
"Good brother, I'm coming," — wild whispering flows;
Pale as a cloud from the grave it rose.

'Twas the harper himself: from the grave he flits;
High on the tombstone the harper sits;
O'er the strings of the cithern his fingers sweep,
And he sings, in a voice right harsh and deep:

"What! know ye yet that song of old,
Which through the heart once deeply rolled,
Ye strings now slow to move?
The angels call it Heaven's joy,
The devils call it Hell's annoy,
But mortals call it—*love!*"

Scarce had sounded the last word's tone,
Ere the graves were opened, every one,
And airy figures came pressing out,
And sweep round the minstrel, while shrill they shout,

"Love, Love, it was thy might
Laid us in these beds with right,

Closed our eyelids from the light:
Wherefore call'st thou in the night?"

So the pack howls bewild'ring, and screeches and
groans,
And roaring and rushing it crackles and moans,
And mad round the minstrel the wild swarm flings,
And wildly his fingers sweep over the strings:

"Bravo! bravo! madder still!
Still welcome be
All, all of ye,
All who mind my magic spell!
Though in little homes of clay
Still as mice long years we lay,
Now we'll drive time merrily on,
If it should please!
First look round!—are we alone?
Fools we were while we were living,
All our souls to madness giving,
To Love's rapturous agonies.
Merry sport to-night can't fail us:
Every one shall truly tell us
What it was of old that drove,
How he was urged,
How he was scourged,
In the crazy hunt of Love!"

As light as the wind from the circle there sprang
A starveling creature, who murmuring sang,

"I was a tailor's journeyman
With needle and with shears;

So quick and slick through work I ran
  With needle and with shears;
But then my master's daughter came,
  With needle and with shears,
And stuck me in my heart, you know,
  With needle and with shears."

Gayly the ghost-laugh went ringing about;
Silent and solemn a second stepped out.

"Bravo Rinaldo Rinaldini,
Schinderhanno, Orlandini,
And Carlo Moor especially,
Were the model men for me.

And I too,—I'm proud to mention,—
Like them, paid to love attention.
A genteel and lovely form
Haunted me quite like a storm.

Then I sighed and sobbed till crazy!
Yes,—till Love had made me hazy:
And—distractedly, I vow—
I picked a pocket, God knows how!

But the beadle grudged that I
Tears of feeling went to dry
With my neighbor's handkerchief,
So he took me—for—a *thief!*

By old catchpoll-custom then,
I was led 'mid armed men,
And the jail so great in grace
Gave a motherly embrace.

With love raptures in my head,
Spinning woolen there I stayed,
Till Rinaldo's shade one day
Took my soul with him away."

Gayly the ghost-laugh went ringing about;
Rouged and bedizened, a third stepped out:

"As a king in the theatre I've thriven,
And played in the first-lover line;
Roaring many a furious 'Oh, Heaven!'
Sighing many a tender 'Love, thine!'

My Mortimer was—what it should be,
And Maria!—her beauty was grand;
But my gestures, though natural as could be,
Never won from the beauty 'a hand:'

Till at last, when despairing completely,
'Maria, thou saint, see me weep!'
And, turning my dagger quite neatly,
I stuck it a trifle too deep."

Gayly the ghost-laugh went ringing about;
In a white wrap-rascal the fourth strolled out:

"In his lecture-chair the professor muddled
And twaddled, and sent me to sleep,—the old quiz!
But I could have slept with more comfort, if cuddled
In bed with that beautiful daughter of his!

From the window her greetings she tenderly showered:
The flower of all flowers,—my life-light so true!

But the flower of the flowers at length was deflowered
By a dry old Philister as rich as a Jew.

Then I cursed all the women and rich old hunkers,
And mixed devil's bitters with wine to stop groans,
And drank friendship with Death until I was as drunk as
The deuce. Says he, 'Right, lad!—my name is Jack Bones!'"

Gayly the ghost-laugh went ringing about;
With a rope round his throttle the fifth walked out:

"The count paraded and boasted o'er wine,
Of his daughter divine, and his jewelry fine;
What care I, count mine, for your diamonds fine?
My taste's for your daughter,—ah, if she were mine!

Both were close under lock and key,—
And the count had many a servant in pay;
But I cared not for servants, for lock, or for key,—
So up on the ladder I went my way.

Up to love's window I clambered fleet,
But heard hard cursing beneath my feet:
'Easy, my boy; give us room on the shelf!
For I have a fancy for jewels myself!'

So the count mocked, and had me bound,
While the swarm of servants came shouting round;
'The devil! D'ye think I'm a thief?' I cried:
'When to steal a sweetheart was all I tried?'

Speech was useless, defence in vain,
The rope was ready, the facts were plain;
And when the sun rose, he wondered to see
A gentleman swing on the gallows-tree."

Gayly the ghost-laugh went ringing about;
With his head in his hands the sixth stepped out:

"Love drove to hunting and to harm,
I roamed with rifle o'er my arm;
A croaking sound came from the tree,
'Heads off!' the raven cried to me.

'If I could only find a dove,
I'd take it home to her I love!'
And so through woods, o'er bush and ground,
My hunter's eye went glancing round.

What bills and coos so soft and fair?
Two turtle-doves are nestling there!
To them with rifle cocked I draw,
And there my own dear love I saw.

My love,—that was the dove I traced,
A stranger her warm form embraced!
Now let your aim, old shot, be good!—
There lay the stranger in his blood.

And soon a train with hangman's fare—
And I the leading person there—
Went through the wood. Up in the oak,
'Heads off!' I heard the raven croak."

Gayly the ghost-laugh went ringing about;
And now the harper himself came out.

"Time was when my song was waking,
The end of my song is come;
When the heart within is breaking,
'Tis time for the songs to go home!"

And doubly maddening the laughter swept;
And up the white phantoms in circles swept,
Till ONE from the belfry came pealing down,
And, howling, each ghost to his grave has gone.

IX.

Ich lag und schlief, und schlief recht mild.

I LAY and slept, and softly slept,
Afar were grief and woe;
And then a dream-form to me swept:
The fairest maid I know.

As pale she seemed as marble stone,
And strangely, wondrous fair;
Her swimming eyes had pearl-like grown,
And dream-like flowed her hair.

And softly, ever softly moved
The maiden marble pale,
And laid her on the heart she loved,
My maiden marble pale.

How beat with pain, with love's sharp zest,
My heart,—how warm it burned!

No throb was in the fair one's breast,—
  To ice that breast was turned.

"No throb, no heat is in my heart,
  As ice I feel it cold;
Yet well I know of love the smart,
  Its power all untold.

"On mouth and lips there glows no red,
  My heart-veins feel no blood;
Yet strive not so with shuddering dread,
  To thee I'm dear and good."

And wilder still she winds me round,
  Half paining, grasping tight;
Loud crow'd the cock,—without a sound
  Forth fled the maiden white.

X.

Da hab' ich viel blasse Leichen.

I'VE called the pale dead round me,
  Full oft by magic might;
And now to themselves they've bound me,
  And will not depart by night.

The spell which the Master taught me
  In my terror no more will come;
And the spectres have well-nigh brought me
  Away to their cloudy home.

Cease, ye black fiends up-swelling!
  Press not around in might!

Why,—rapture perhaps is dwelling
  Up here in a rosy light!

I must strive, while life beats through me,
  For the beautiful flower life bore;
What value had all life to me
  Could I love that flower no more?

And oh that I once could capture
  And hold her embraced again,
And her lips and cheeks in rapture
  Kiss wildly with life's sweet pain!

And that once from her mouth, though sadly,
  A word of love might come!
Ah, then, ye grim ghosts, how gladly
  I'd pass to your terrible home!

They have heard my vow, and they hold me,
  And bow to it fearfully;
Loved heart, for thy love I have sold me!
  Loved heart! say,—oh, lovest thou *me?*

Songs.

I.

Morgens steh' ich auf und frage.

WHEN night flies, I ask the morrow,
Comes my love to-day?
Then at eve I yield to sorrow,
Yet another day!

And the night with little sleeping,
But with grief enough, is gone;
Half asleep, my sorrow keeping,
Through the day I wander on.

II.

Es treibt mich hin, es treibt mich her.

NOW here, now there I'm urged—at last!
But a few hours to wait, and, oh, then I shall meet her,
The fairest of maidens,—and soon I shall greet her:
O faithful heart, why this beating so fast?

Oh, but the hours are a lazy pack!
  Strolling at their ease, and idle;
  Rolling, yawning, how they sidle
To each other!—run, you pack!

Raging impatience is driving me fast;
  Surely the hours were never love-plighted,
  Since in a cruel sly compact united
They spitefully mock at all true lovers' haste.

III.

Ich wandelte unter den Bäumen.

ALL under the trees I wandered,
  I with my grief alone;
There came the old dreams as I pondered,
  And into my heart went down.

Who taught ye that spell on my spirit,
  Birds, high o'er the wind and the rain?
Be still!—if my heart should but hear it,
  'Twould cost it full many a pain.

"All under the greenwood walking,
  A maiden singing we heard:
So we birds repeat in our talking
  That beautiful golden word."

No more from your memory borrow:
  Too much for a small bird you know;
You fain would be stealing my sorrow,
  But *I* trust in nobody,—no!

IV.

Lieb' Liebchen, leg's Händchen auf's Herze mein.

LOVE, my love,—lay your small hand on my heart,
Hear, every second a beat and a start!
There dwells a carpenter,—evil is he,—
Always at work on a coffin for me.

He hammers by night, and he hammers by day;
Long he has driven my sleep far away;
Hammer, old carpenter, hammer your best!
So that I quickly may go to my rest.

V.

Schöne Wiege meiner Leiden.

LOVELY cradle of my sorrow,
Lovely tomb of peace to me.
Lovely town, we part to-morrow,—
And farewell I cry to thee!

Sacred home,—you'll see me never,
Never more where she has strayed;
Home, farewell!—we part forever,
Where I first beheld the maid.

Had there only been no meeting,
Queen of hearts, with you, I vow,
I should not be thus repeating
That I feel so wretched now.

I ne'er sought to win and wear you,
And I asked not for your faith;

But in peace to live, and near you,
  Where the breezes caught your breath.

You yourself did force this parting,
  Bitter words I heard you speak;
And with madness through me darting,
  All my heart is sore and weak.

And with limbs both weak and weary,
  With my travelling staff I'll go,
Till the grave, all still, though dreary,
  Gives me rest in lands below.

VI.

Warte, warte, wilder Schiffsmann.

WAIT, oh, wait, impatient sailor!
  Fast enough my footsteps stir;
From two maidens I am parting,—
  From Europa, and from her.

And may blood, in streams, burst from me!
  Blood, in streams, come dim my sight!
That with blood, and all hot burning,
  I my anguish down may write.

Ah, my dearest!—why this mourning?
  Shudderest thou my blood to see?
When all pale and heart a-bleeding,
  Years—long years—I stood by thee!

Know'st thou not the ancient ballad
  Of the snake in Paradise,

Who by evil gift of apples
  Drove our ancestor to vice?

Apples brought us every evil,
  EVE, with apples, brought us death;
ERIS brought the flames to Ilium,—
  Thou didst bring both flames and death.

VII.

Berg' und Burgen schau'n herunter.

HILLS and towers are gazing downward
  In the mirror-gleaming Rhine,
And my boat drives gayly onward,
  While the sun-rays round it shine.

Calm I watch the wavelets stealing,
  Golden gleaming, as I glide;
Calmly too awakes the feeling
  Which within my heart I hide.

Gently greeting and assuring,
  Bright the river tempts me on;
Well I know that face alluring!
  Death and night lie further down!

Joy above, at heart beguiling,—
  Thou'rt my own love's image, Flood!
She too knows the art of smiling,
  She can seem as calm and good.

VIII.

Anfangs wollt' ich fast verzagen.

I AT first was near despairing;
Never hoped to endure as now,
And at length the whole I'm bearing;
Only, do not ask me how.

IX.

Mit Rosen, Cypressen und Flittergold.

WITH roses, with cypress, and gold leaf bright,*
Fain would I cover, lovely and light,
This book of mine, like a coffin thin,
And bury my songs like a corpse therein.

And, oh, could I bury this love in repose!
The flower of quiet on love's grave grows:
There it blooms, and is plucked when full and high;
But mine will ne'er blossom till buried I lie.

For here are the songs which so wildly rose,
Wildly as Etna his lava throws;
Up they burst from my soul's abyss,
Mad was their flame with its sparkle and hiss.

Now they lie dumb as the dead in their shrouds,
Now they stare coldly and white as the clouds;

---

* In allusion to the curious German custom of adorning the dead with leaf gold as well as flowers.

Yet the glow from their ashes to life would leap,
If the spirit of love should over them sweep.

And feelings prophetic within me say
That love's spirit will melt o'er them yet some day,
If this book should ever come to thy hand,
Thou dearest love in a distant land.

And then from the spell of song set free,
The death-white letters shall look at thee;
Look in thy beautiful eyes with prayer,
And sorrow and love will be whispering there.

Romances.

I.

THE MOURNER.

Allen thut es weh im Herzen.

EVERY tender heart shows feeling,
When that pale boy comes again:
For the sorrow he's concealing,
In his face is written plain.

And the pitying breezes greet him,
Fanning cool his burning brow;
And the once proud girls who meet him
Kindly would console him now.

From the cities' roar and bustle,
Now he seeks the forest bounds;
Merrily the green leaves rustle,
Merrily the bird-song sounds.

But the song soon has an ending:
Sadly rustle leaf and tree
When, all slowly woodward tending,
The pale, mournful boy they see.

II.

THE MOUNTAIN ECHO.

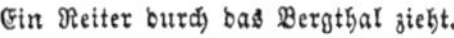
Ein Reiter durch das Bergthal zieht.

A RIDER through the valley passed,
And sang a mournful stave,—
"And ride I hence to my true love's arms,
Or to a gloomy grave?"
The rocks an echo gave:
"A gloomy grave!"

And onward rode the cavalier,
And still his sighs increase;
"So I must away to an early grave!
Well, then,—the grave hath peace."
The echo would not cease:
"The grave hath peace."

And from the rider's care-worn cheek
A single tear there fell;
"And if only the grave has peace for me,
Why, then,—in the grave all's well!"
The echo gave a knell,—
"In the grave all's well!"

III.

TWO BROTHERS.

Oben auf der Bergesspitze.

ON yon mountain-summit dreaming,
Wrapped in night, dim towers lie;

In the valley lights are gleaming,
  Shining swords in combat fly.

Those are brothers who are fighting;
  Grim the strife as fury's brand:
Why are brothers' quarrels righting
  With the rapier in the hand?

Countess Laura's bright eyes burning
  Lit the brothers' rage, 'tis said.
Both were drunk with love, and burning
  For the noble, lovely maid.

But for whom has she decided?
  Whither turns her heart? but now
All debate is still divided,—
  Sword, flash out!—decide it thou!

Madly now they fight despairing,
  Cut on cut with crashing might;
But beware, ye blades so daring!
  Devilish spells flit round by night!

Woe, oh, woe! each cruel brother!
  Woe! thou bloody vale of ill!
Each leaps headlong at the other,
  Dying on the other's steel!

Centuries like mists have faded,
  Many an ancient race is flown;
Still in the mountain's darkest shadow
  Sad the empty tower looks down.

But by night, deep in the valley,
When dim forms sweep strangely round,
Forth to fight the brothers sally
When they hear the midnight sound.

IV.

POOR PETER.

1.

Der Hans und die Grete tanzen herum.

JACK and his Maggie go dancing around,
Shouting like merry mad creatures;
Peter is standing all dumb on the ground,
Whiter than chalk are his features.

Jack and his Maggie are bridegroom and bride,
Their gay wedding-garments displaying;
Peter is gnawing his nails all aside,
And round in his working-dress straying.

Peter speaks slowly and sad from his heart,
As he sees how the fond couple go it;
"Ah! if I were not just a *little* too smart,
I should do myself mischief,—I know it!"

2.

In meiner Brust da sitzt ein Weh.

DEEP in my breast's a pain alway,
Until my breast seems bursting;
And where I stay, or where I stray,
It's driving me and thrusting.

It drives me to the girl I prize,
  As if I thought she'd cure it;
But when I look her in the eyes,
  I go,—and still endure it.

I climb away to the mountain-top,
  Where no man hears me sighing;
And then, when still up there I stop,—
  Stop still,—and go to crying.

3.

Der arme Peter wankt vorbei.

POOR Peter wanders, tottering, by,
Pale as a corpse, and slow and shy;
And those who see him in the street,
Amazed, half check their rapid feet.

Girls whisper in each other's ear,
"He's risen from the grave, it's clear."
My gentle girls, you're wrong, I know:
He's hastening to the grave below.

He's lost his love, and all seems dim;
The grave's the proper place for him,—
The fittest place his head to lay,
And slumber till the judgment-day.

V.

SONG OF THE PRISONER.

Als meine Großmutter die Lise behext.

FOLKS said, when my granny Eliza bewitched,
  She must burn for her horrid transgression;
Much ink from his pen the old magistrate pitched,
  But he could not extort a confession.

And when in the kettle my granny was thrown,
  She yelled death and murder while dying;
And when the black smoke all around us was blown,
  As a raven she rose and went flying.

Little black grandmother feathered so well,
  Oh, come to the tower where I'm sitting;
Bring cakes and bring cheese to me here in the cell,
  Through the iron-barred window flitting.

Little black grandmother feathered and wise,
  Just give my aunt a warning;
Lest she should come fluttering and pick out my eyes
  When I merrily swing in the morning.

VI.

THE GRENADIERS.

Nach Frankreich zogen zwei Grenadier.

TO the land of France went two grenadiers,
  From a Russian prison returning;
But they hung down their heads on the German frontiers,
  The news from their fatherland learning.

For there they both heard the sorrowful tale
  That France was by fortune forsaken;
That her mighty army was scattered like hail,
  And the Emperor, the Emperor taken.

Then there wept together the grenadiers,
  The sorrowful story learning;
And one said, "Oh, woe!" as the news he hears,
  "How I feel my old wound burning!"

The other said, "The song is sung,
  And I wish that we both were dying!
But at home I've a wife and a child—they're young—
  On me, and me only, relying.

Yet what is a wife or a child to me?
  Deeper wants all my spirit have shaken:
Let them beg, let them beg, should they hungry be!
  My Emperor, my Emperor taken!

But I beg you, brother, if by chance
  You soon shall see me dying,
Then take my corpse with you back to France,—
  Let it ever in France be lying.

The cross of honor with crimson band
  Shall rest on my heart as it bound me;
Give me my musket in my hand,
  And buckle my sword around me.

And there I will lie and listen still,
  In my sentry-coffin staying,
Till I feel the thundering cannon's thrill,
  And horses trampling and neighing.

Then my Emperor will ride, well over my grave,
  Mid sabres bright slashing and smiting;
And I'll rise all weaponed up out of my grave,—
  For the Emperor, the Emperor fighting."*

VII.

THE MESSAGE.

Mein Knecht! steh' auf und sattle schnell.

"NOW rise, my squire, and saddle quick,
  Ride fast o'er lea and lands,
Through greenwood fair and field, to where
  King Duncan's castle stands.

"Then slip into the stall, and wait
  Till thou some groom hast spied;
And ask for me, 'Say, who may be
  Of Duncan's daughters bride?'

"And should he say, 'The brown girl weds,'
  Then bring the news in haste;
But if he says, 'The light-haired maid,'
  You need not ride so fast.

"Then go to Master Ropemaker,
  And buy for me a cord;
Ride slowly back, and bring it me,
  And never speak a word."

---

* The best translation of this lyric which I have met with is that of the Rev. W. H. FURNESS, given in his *Gems of German Verse*, Philadelphia: Hazard, 1860. C. G. L.

VIII.

TAKING HOME THE BRIDE.

Ich geh' nicht allein, mein feines Lieb'.

"I GO not alone, my dainty love;
Away with me thou'lt wander
To the dear known, gray old, dreary retreat,
To the sad, lone, stone-cold, wearisome seat,
Where my mother is lurking crouched up by the door,
And waits till her son returns once more."

"Leave me alone, thou gloomy man:
Who has called thee hither?
Thy breath is a-glow, thine eyes beam bright,
Thy hand is snow, and thy cheek is white,
But I will merrily pass the time
Mid rose-perfume in a sunny clime."

"Let roses breathe perfume, let sunbeams shine on,
My sweetest darling!
Vail thee in broad-spread, white wavering attire,
Sweep every thread of the quavering lyre,
And sing out our wedding song for me;
The night-wind shall whistle the melody!"

IX.

DON RAMIRO.

Donna Clara, Donna Clara.

"DONNA Clara! Donna Clara!
Thou for many years my dearest,

Hast determined on my ruin,
  Caring not though death be near me.

"Donna Clara! Donna Clara!
  Life of all our gifts is sweetest;
But our death's a grisly spectre,
  And the grave is cold and cheerless.

"Donna Clara! smile,—to-morrow
  Don Fernando at the altar
Will as loving bridegroom greet thee:
  Bid me to thy wedding, Clara!"

"Don Ramiro! Don Ramiro!
  What thou sayest wounds me sorely,—
Deeper than the cruel sentence
  Which the unyielding stars keep o'er me.

"Don Ramiro, Don Ramiro,
  Cease, oh, cease this dismal grieving:
In this world are many maidens;
  God himself forbids our meeting.

"Don Ramiro, thou who bravely
  Many a Moor in war hast vanquished,
O'er thyself now gain a victory,
  Come to-morrow to my marriage."

"Donna Clara! Donna Clara!
  Yes,—I swear it on my honor,—
I will come. We'll dance together.—
  Love, good-night: I come to-morrow."

"Love, good-night!" The window rattled,
  Sighing stood Ramiro near it,
Stood like stone,—at last departed,
  In the darkness disappearing.

And at last, their combat over,
  Morning drives his foeman, darkness,
And Toledo lies outspreading,
  Like a variegated garden.

Many a glorious house and palace
  In the sunshine brightly glittered,
And the domes of stately churches
  Shone in splendor, as if gilded.

Like a swarm of bees far humming,
  Sound the festal bells sweet tolling;
Gently chimes the choral music,
  From the churches softly flowing.

And behold how blithely yonder,
  Yonder from the great cathedral,
Gay in tumult and in turmoil,
  All the gorgeous crowd is streaming!

Knights in armor, graceful ladies,
  Courtiers ever bowing, smiling;
Organ-music deeply rolling,
  Church-bells in the pauses chiming.

But with deep respect the many
  Round one vacant spot still wander,
Giving place to bride and bridegroom:
  Donna Clara, Don Fernando.

To the bridegroom's palace-portal
  Still the eager crowd advances;
Here the bridal feast commences,
  In the grand old Spanish manner.

Knightly games and merry banquets
  Pass in turn, mid cheers and laughter;
Hours fly on, forgot in revelling,
  Till the night falls dark and darker.

Till the guests are met for dancing,
  Still the bride and groom attending;
Mid a thousand lamps their garments
  Shine in many colors splendid.

High on chairs above the many,
  Bride and bridegroom sit together,
Donna Clara, Don Fernando,
  Whispering words both soft and gentle.

Warlike in the hall around them,
  All the glittering guests are sweeping;
Loud the kettle-drums are ringing,
  And the trumpets loudly pealing.

"But, I beg you, say, my dearest,
  Why your glances are directed
Ever to the corner yonder?"
  Said Fernando in amazement.

"Who is that, in deep black mantle?
  Whose that form?—say, Don Fernando!"
But the cavalier, loud laughing,
  Said, "Why, that?—'tis but a shadow!"

But it was a human figure.
  Slowly came the cloaked one sweeping:
'Twas Ramiro. To him Clara
  Blushing gave a friendly greeting.

And the dance again beginning,
  Wilder still the crowd goes sweeping;
Wilder all the waltzers whirling,
  Till the very floor is creaking.

"Very gladly, Don Ramiro,
  Will I join with you the dancers;
But you should not to my wedding
  Come in such a night-black mantle."

With a fearful, fixed expression
  At the lady gazed Ramiro;
As his arm he wound about her,
  Hoarse he said, "You bade me hither!"

In the whirling, dancing tumult
  Now the waltzing pair are pressing;
Loud the kettle-drums are rattling,
  And the trumpets' peal is deafening.

"Why, thy cheeks are white as marble!"
  Clara whispered, half in terror.
"It was *you* who bade me hither,"
  Fell Ramiro's voice in echo.

In the hall the torches flicker,
  Everywhere the crowd is flowing;
And the kettle-drums are rattling,
  And the trumpets sternly roaring.

"And your hands, like ice, are freezing!"
  Whispered Clara, horror-gasping;
"It was you who bade me hither:"—
  Through the tumult still they're dashing.

"Leave me, leave me! Don Ramiro!
  Corpse-like is thy breath, and chilling;"
And the hollow voice still answered,
  "It was you who called me hither!"

Smoke-like seems the floor, and glowing,
  Merrily harp and viol playing;
In a maddening, magic twining,
  All things in the hall seem fading.

"Leave me, leave me! Don Ramiro!"
  Closer, wavelike press the figures;
Don Ramiro ever answering,
  "It was you who called me hither!"

"Then, I say, in GOD's name, leave me!"
  Clara firmly cried, though anxious;
Scarcely was the word outspoken,
  When at once Ramiro vanished.

Pale as death, and stiffly staring,
  Lost in darkness, Clara shivered;
FRANCE had through her gloomy kingdom
  With the pure white spirit flitted.

Now the mighty slumber passes,
  Now the lids again are opening;
But new wonder pressing on her
  Tempts again those eyes to closing.

For since first the dance assembled,
  From her chair she had not risen:
She is sitting by her bridegroom,
  And Fernando anxious whispers,

"Say, what pales those cheeks, my dearest?
  Why that ghastly dim expression?"
"*And Ramiro?*"—stammered Clara,
  And her tongue was checked with terror.

On the bridegroom's brow a shadow
  Fell,—dark thoughts his soul absorbing.
"Lady, probe not bloody rumors:
  Don Ramiro died this morning."

X.

BELSHAZZAR.

Die Mitternacht zog näher schon;
In stummer Ruh' lag Babylon.

MIDNIGHT came slowly sweeping on;
  In silent rest lay Babylon.

But in the royal castle high
Red torches gleam and courtiers cry.

Belshazzar there in kingly hall
Is holding kingly festival.

The vassals sat in glittering line,
And emptied the goblets with glowing wine.

The goblets rattle, the choruses swell,
And it pleased the stiff-necked monarch well.

In the monarch's cheeks a wild fire glowed,
And the wine awoke his daring mood.

And, onward still by his madness spurred,
He blasphemes the LORD with a sinful word.

And he brazenly boasts, blaspheming wild,
While the servile courtiers cheered and smiled.

Quick the king spoke, while his proud glance burned,
Quickly the servant went and returned.

He bore on his head the vessels of gold,
Of Jehovah's temple the plunder bold.

With daring hand, in his frenzy grim,
The king seized a beaker and filled to the brim,

And drained to the dregs the sacred cup,
And foaming he cried, as he drank it up,

"Jehovah, eternal scorn I own
To thee. I am monarch of Babylon."

Scarce had the terrible blasphemy rolled
From his lips, ere the monarch at heart was cold.

The yelling laughter was hushed, and all
Was still as death in the royal hall.

And see! and see! on the white wall high
The form of a hand went slowly by,

And wrote,—and wrote, on the broad wall white,
Letters of fire, and vanished in night.

Pale as death, with a steady stare,
And with trembling knees, the king sat there.

The horde of slaves sat shuddering chill;
No word they spoke, but were deathlike still.

The Magians came, but of them all,
None could read the flame-script on the wall.

But that same night, in all his pride,
By the hands of his servants Belshazzar died.

XI.

THE MINNESINGERS.

Zu dem Wettgesange schreiten.

TO the strife of song forth wending
  See the Minnesingers bent;
Ah! there is a strange contending,
  And a right strange tournament!

Foaming FANTASIE wild rearing
  Is the Minnesinger's steed;
Art is all the shield he's bearing,
  And his word his sword indeed!

On the gay-decked terrace flaunting,
  Lovely dames look gayly down;
But the right one still is wanting,
  And the proper laurel-crown.

Other warriors when springing
  In the tourney-lists are sound,

But we minstrel-knights come bringing
  Here with us our deadliest wound.

And he there from whom comes springing
  Blood of songs from the heart's deeps,
He is victor,—he is bringing
  Best of praise to loveliest lips.

XII.

LOOKING FROM THE WINDOW.

Der bleiche Heinrich ging vorbei.

PALE Henry caught fair Hedwig's eye;
  She never dreamed he'd hear it,
So said, as he went walking by,
  "He's white as any spirit!"

Then Henry raised his glance above,
  Quite longingly,—or near it;
It made fair Hedwig sigh for love,
  And pale as any spirit.

From window-gazing, days she stayed,
  Till blood no more could bear it;
So, now she sleeps by him in bed,
  Like any girl of spirit.

XIII.

THE WOUNDED KNIGHT.

Ich weiß eine alte Kunde.

I KNOW a mournful reading
  Of a tale no longer new,

How a knight in love lies bleeding
  For a love no longer true.

Now he must deem ungrateful
  The one who holds his heart,
And he must hold as hateful
  His love with bitter smart.

He would fain in the lists go riding,
  And call forth the knights to strife:
"Let any my love deriding
  Come answer the charge with his life!"

Then no answer will be given,
  Save by his own deep smart;
So his lance-point must be driven
  At his own accusing heart.

XIV.

THE VOYAGE.

Ich stand gelehnet an den Mast,
Und zählte jede Welle.

I COUNTED every falling wave,
  While leaning on the mast:
Adieu, my own dear fatherland!
  My ship is sailing fast.

I sailed before my dear love's house,
  Bright gleamed each window-pane;
There is no sign for me to-night,
  I look and look in vain.

Keep from my eyes, ye bitter tears,
  Lest I too dimly see!
And thou, weak heart,—oh, do not break,
  In this stern agony!

XV.

THE BALLAD OF RUE.

Herr Ulrich reitet im grünen Wald.

SIR Ulrich in the green wood rides,
  The merry leaves' rustle hearing;
A lovely form before him glides,
  Through distant branches peering.

The young knight says, "I know full well
  That form all blooming, glowing;
In crowded street, in lonely dell,
  It flits where'er I'm going.

"Two roses are yon rosy lips,
  So fresh and fair I've seen them;
Yet many a hateful word oft slips
  Right treacherously between them.

"And so that mouth, so soft and sly,
  A rose-tree is recalling,
Where poisonous serpents, wondrous sly,
  'Neath dark-green leaves are crawling.

"Each dimple in her cheeks engraved,
  In wondrous lovely fashion,
Are graves indeed, where as I raved
  I fell through headlong passion.

"And those fair locks of flowing hair,
Which float in dreams around me,
Those are the nets so wondrous fair
Wherewith the devil bound me.

"And those deep eyes of heavenly blue
As though calm fountains drowned them,
I deemed them heaven's own gates so true,
The gates of hell I found them."

Sir Ulrich through the green wood rides,
Leaves rustle grimly o'er him;
A second form afar there glides,
So pale and sad, before him.

The young knight says, "O mother dear,
Whose mother-love would not leave me,
Though I with deed and word of fear
So long and bitterly grieved thee.

"Could I dry those weeping eyes so meek
With the burning fire of sorrow,
And could I, to redden that pale white cheek,
The blood from my own heart borrow!"

Sir Ulrich rides the forest bound,
Darker the wood is growing;
Strange voices all are rising round,
The night-wind whispering, flowing.

The young knight hears his own sad words,
Repeated, echo o'er him;
That was the mocking wild-wood birds,
Who chirruped and sang before him.

Sir Ulrich on his way doth wend,
  The Ballad of Rue still singing,
And when he has sung it to an end,
  You may hear him again beginning.

XVI.

TO A LADY SINGER,

AS SHE SANG AN OLD BALLAD.

Ich denke noch der Zaubervollen,
Wie sie zuerst mein Auge sah!

EVEN now, as when I first beheld her,
  Her magic seems my soul to melt!
How full of love was all her singing,
So sweetly in my heart deep ringing!
How tears into my eyes came springing,—
And yet I knew not how I felt.

A dream came gently stealing o'er me;
As though once more a happy child;
I still sat by the small lamp's gleaming,
In mother's dear, kind room a-dreaming,
Reading a tale with wonders teeming,
While dark without the storm blew wild.

A real life stole o'er the story,
Old knights came rising from the grave;
At Roncesvalles was gallant fighting!
On rode brave Roland, death inviting;
Bold knights around him sternly smiting
And Ganelon,—alas!—the knave!

By him to sad death-sleep came Roland,
Gasping in blood at life's extreme.
Scarce could his bugle-notes far pealing
Reach Charlemagne o'er wide leagues stealing.
Now he lies dead,—devoid of feeling;—
And with him dies away my dream.

Then came a loud bewildering clamor,
Away, away the visions sweep:
The legend vanished mid a rapping,
The audience their hands were clapping,
And loud their cries of *brava!* snapping;
The lovely singer courtsied deep.

XVII.

SONG OF THE DUCATS.

Meine gülbenen Dukaten,
Sagt, wo seid ihr hingerathen?

O MY golden ducats! say,
Whither are you gone away?

Are ye with the golden fishes
Who in the river gayly thriving
Up go leaping, down go diving?

Are ye with the golden flowers
Which on the green vale, sweet to view,
Glitter clear in morning dew?

Are ye with the golden birdlings
Which, through sun-rays web-like twining,
Sweeping in the blue go shining?

Are ye with the golden planets,
To the constellations given,
Smiling every night from heaven?

Ah, my glittering ducats golden,
In the waves ye do not swim,
On the greensward do not gleam,
In blue air ye do not sweep,
Nor glittering smile from heaven deep;
For my creditors*—good cause!—
Hold you tightly in their claws.

XVIII.

DIALOGUE ON THE PADERBORN HEATH.

Hörst Du nicht die fernen Töne?

"HEAR'ST thou not far music ringing,
Viol sweet, and organ sounding?
Many a lovely form is springing
In yon elf-dance flitting, bounding."

---

* Meine Manichäer, traun!
Halten Euch in ihren Klau'n,

"Manichäer." At the German universities creditors or duns are termed Manichæans, after the well-known sect of that name. The term of reproach was evidently borrowed at an early age, when much was said in theological lectures against heretics. The student legend is that the Manichæans were Persian Magi, who were importunate in collecting the money due them for exercising their art.

„Laßt die Manichäer immer klopfen,
Ich verriegle meine Stubenthür';
Der Gestank von solchen Wiedehopfen
Kommt den Burschen ganz verteufelt für."

[*Note by Translator.*]

"How, my friend? your mind must wander,
  Or my hearing's strangely blunted:
I can hear no fiddling yonder;
  Only swine which just now grunted."

"Hear'st thou not the bugle pealing?
  Hunters blithe through greenwood straying,
Lambs I see o'er meadows stealing,
  Shepherds on their reed pipes playing."

"Ah, my friend, your ears are humming:
  There's no pipe or bugle pealing;
I but see a swineherd coming,
  And before him pigs a-squealing."

"Hear'st thou not melodious measure,
  As a strife of voices singing?
Angels hear it, rapt in pleasure,
  Beating time on pinions swinging."

"That which seemed to you so pleasant
  Was no heavenly minstrels' striving;
Friend, it's just a little peasant
  Singing as his geese he's driving!"

"Hear'st thou church-bells as if talking,
  Sweetly, strangely, wildly flowing?
See the congregation walking,
  Calmly to the chapel going!"

"Ah, my friend, it's but the tinkling
  From the distant cow-bells given,
As the kine, by starlight twinkling,
  Slowly to their stalls are driven."

"See yon fluttering veil,—oh, wonder!
  See,—a beckoning form advances!
'Tis my loved one standing yonder,
  Tearful sorrow in her glances!"

"Ah, my friend, she who approaches
  Is Old Liz, from the wood's shadow;
Pale and tottering on her crutches,
  She goes limping towards the meadow."

"Smile, dear friend, that so I borrow
  Forms for such fantastic seeming:
Oh that all my heart's deep sorrow
  Thou couldst turn to idle dreaming!"

XIX.

LIFE-GREETING.

[AN ALBUM-LEAF.]

Eine große Landstraß' ist unsere Erd'.

THIS earth of ours is a great highway,
  We mortals are passengers greeting;
We hurry on horseback or foot all day,
  Like runners or couriers fleeting.

We pass each other, we nod and we twist,
  Waving handkerchiefs from the wagon;
We had gladly embraced or had gladly kissed,
  But the horses their loads must drag on.

We scarce at one station each other knew,
Alexander, dear prince and brother,
Ere loud the postilion his bugle blew,
And blew us away from each other.

XX.

NO, INDEED!

Wenn der Frühling kommt mit dem Sonnenschein.

WHEN spring is coming with sun-rays bright,
Budding and blooming each floweret creeps;
While the moon o'er her course of glory sweeps,
And the stars swim after in floods of light;
When the poet sees two sweet eyes aglow,
From his deepest soul the songs out-flow;—
But songs and stars and pleasant flowers,
And eyes and moon-gleams and sunny hours,
Much as this stuff may please us all,
Don't go far to make up this earthly ball.

TO A. W. VON SCHLEGEL.

Im Reifrockputz, mit Blumen reich verzieret.

IN wide-hooped dress and flowers of gaudy brightness,
With well-rouged cheeks, and beauty-spots, well-scented,
In pointed shoes with broidery ornamented,
With high head-dress, and laced to wasp-like tightness,
So seemed the Mock-Muse, in rococo fashion,
Seeking thy warm embraces when she saw thee;
But from her path thou quickly didst withdraw thee,
And wandered on, driven by dreaming passion.
In the wild waste a tower thou didst discover,
And, like a fair white statue in its keeping,
A lovely maid in magic spells lay sleeping;
But the charm vanished at thy kiss, O rover!
The *real* German muse woke to her lover,
And sank into thy arms, with rapture weeping.

TO MY MOTHER, B. HEINE,

NÉE VON GELDERN.

I.

Ich bin's gewöhnt, den Kopf recht hoch zu tragen.

IT is my wont my head right high to carry,
Impatiently the slightest crosses bearing:
If the king's self into my eyes were staring,
My gaze upon his own as long would tarry.
But, mother dear, I do confess before you,
Whatever puffed-up pride comes on me stealing,
In your sweet presence I do lose that feeling,
And then a trembling diffidence falls o'er me:
Is it your soul with mine all strangely blending,
Your higher soul all things before it bending,
In lightning gleams upwards to heaven tending?
Does memory torture me because I proved you
With many a deed which once so sadly moved you,
Moved that dear heart which ever dearly loved me?

II.

Im tollen Wahn hatt' ich Dich einst verlassen.

IN wild delusion from thy side once turning,
I wished to roam at will the whole world over;
I wished to see if love would greet the rover,
And quench with Love the Love within me burning.
Through every street I sought, false Hope beguiling,
At every gate I stretched my hands in sorrow;
Not the least love-gift could I beg or borrow,—
They only gave me *hate*, cold hate, while smiling.

So ever on I went for Love, and ever,
And still for Love, yet Love approached me never,
And so turned home again, all sick in sorrow.
Then thou didst come to me with eyes all beaming;
And, oh, what was it in those dear eyes gleaming
But the sweet longed-for Love I could not borrow?

TO H. S.

Wie ich Dein Büchlein hastig aufgeschlagen.

I OPED thy book in haste, and, lo, before me
There strangely swept familiar forms long banished,
The golden pictures which for years had vanished,
That in my boyhood's dreams and days swept o'er me.
Again I see, proudly to heaven up-raying,
The good cathedral, built by faith availing,—
By German faith,—and hear a sweet love-wailing
Amid the tones of bells and organ playing.
I see right well, too, on the temple tripping,
The daring dwarfs go hammering and shaking,
The lovely tracery and flower-work breaking;
But though men work for aye, the old oak stripping,
Of all their verdant spoil his limbs bereaving,
When the spring comes, afresh ye'll find him leaving.

FRESCO SONNETS TO CHRISTIAN SETHE.

1.

Ich tanz' nicht mit, ich räuch're nicht den Klötzen.

I DANCE not with, I worship not, that rabble
 Who are all gold without, within all sand;
 I'm not urbane when a knave holds out his hand,
Who secretly my name with filth would dabble;
Nor do I bow to those fair dames who drabble
 Their names with pride through all the shame i' the land.
 I drag no burdens when the mob hath spanned
Its idol's chariot with acclaiming gabble.
 I know the oak must on the ground be lying,
 While the brook-reed once bent goes upward flying,
After the storm, elastic as before.
And yet what is the reed when all is o'er?
 How lucky! first as cane it serves some dandy,
 Then to dust clothes his boot-black finds it handy.

2.

Gieb' her die Larv' — ich will mich jetzt maskiren.

GIVE me that mask,—for masked I'll cross the border
 Of Rascaldom, that rascals with me walking,
 Who splendidly "in character" go stalking,
May not imagine I am of their order.
Of vulgar words and modes I'll be recorder,
 Like the vile mob, in their own language talking;
 Bright gems of wit no more will I go hawking,
Such as each coxcomb sports in gay disorder.

So through the great masked ball I will go bounding·
Mid German knights, monks, monarchs high respected,
Greeted by harlequins,—by none detected,—
Their swords of lath upon my jacket sounding.
And there's the joke. If off my mask were taken,
With what still horror would the pack be shaken!

3.

Ich lache ob den abgeschmackten Laffen.

LOUDLY I laugh at the dry, soulless flunkey
Who stares around him with his goat-grimaces;
I laugh at the tyros, too, with sober faces,
Snuffling and piping ever on their one key;
I laugh, too, at the over-learned monkey,
Who vaunts himself a judge of all the graces;
I laugh at the coward, iron-headed donkey,
Who threatens poisoned steel, and all disgraces!
When Fortune's seven fair gifts are gone, and after
We see how Fate's grim threatening finger quivers,
The last dear fragments ruined round us lying,
And when the very heart within is dying,
Dying and hacked and torn to wretched shivers,
What then remains save broad and bitter laughter?

4.

Im Hirn spuckt mir ein Mährchen wunderfein.

MY brain is haunted by a legend rare,
And' in the tale a wondrous ballad rings,
And in the song there lives and blooms and springs
A wondrous winsome little maiden fair.

And the maid with her a small heart, too, brings;
But ah, that heart! no love is glowing there;
In that cold soul, frosty beyond compare,
Grim Pride alone, or more than Pride, still sings:
Hear how it hums in my head, this noisy wonder!
How my brain beats, as though 'twould rend my forehead!
And how the maiden titters, as if playing!
I only fear my head may burst asunder;
And, oh!—but then the very thought is horrid,—
What if my mind from its beaten track went straying!

5.

Im stiller, wehmuthweicher Abendstunde.

WHEN still soft evening hours are sadly going,
And long-forgotten songs blend with my dreaming,
And tears adown my cheeks again are streaming,
And from my old heart's wound the blood comes flowing,
And when, as in a magic mirror gleaming,
I see HER form slowly to likeness growing,
In a red bodice at her table sewing,
All in her happy sphere so silent seeming,—
When suddenly she from her chair upspringing
Cuts from her locks the loveliest of tresses,
And gives it me,—the rapture half distresses;
But, oh, the devil comes, his torture bringing;
From those fair hairs a binding rope he's twisted,
And now for years has dragged me as he listed.

6.

Als ich vor einem Jahr Dich wiederblickte.

"WHEN I saw thee again in last year's meeting,
Thou didst not kiss a welcome on that day!"
As I said this, my love, in pretty play,
With sweetest kiss gave to my lips a greeting,
Then plucked—an instant from my side retreating—
A myrtle-twig which in the window lay:
"Take this," she said, "plant it without delay,
And place a glass on it."—Oh, love-gift fleeting!
'Twas all long, long ago. The twig is dead;
For years I have not seen the maid I wooed;
And yet the kiss burns wildly in my head;
And lately from afar it drove me on
To where she dwells. Before the house I stood,
The whole night long, nor left till morning shone.

7.

Hüt Dich, mein Freund, vor grimmen Teufelsfratzen.

BEWARE, my friend, of devilish grins and glaring,
Yet worse are the soft smiles of angel-hussies;
One offered me of late the sweetest busses,
But when she came I felt sharp claws and daring.
Beware, too, of old cats, spitting and swearing.
And yet much worse are snow-white tender pussies:
I caught one late for a pet, with cunning ruses,
But soon my Pussy at my heart was tearing.
O honey hussy,—beautiful offender!

How could thy glances for my love so angle?
How could thy pretty paws my heart so mangle?
O pussy-Katrine's pretty paws so tender,
Oh, I would kiss thee, love, without receding,
Though all the while my heart were clawed and bleeding.

8.

Du sah'st mich oft im Kampf mit jenen Schlingeln.

THOU'ST seen me oft with knaves in altercation,
With puppies spectacled and tabbies painted,
Who my good name have any thing but sainted,
Or rather sought to sink it to damnation.
Thou saw'st me bored by pedants' affectation,
How fools their caps and bells came round me rattling,
How poisonous serpents round my heart were battling,
And how it bled till courage well-nigh fainted.
But thou wert ever firm, like a great tower;
Thy head my beacon was in the stormy hour,
Thy trusty heart a haven safe and sure;
'Tis true, wild storms around that port are flying,
And few the ships within its shelter lying,
But he who once is there may rest secure.

9.

Ich möchte weinen, doch ich kann es nicht.

I WOULD be weeping, yet I cannot weep;
I fain would bravely far on high go springing,
And yet can not; to the ground I must be clinging,
While serpents vile around me hiss and creep;
And fain would I over them all go sweep,
That light of life, my love, to glory bringing,
In her all-blessed breath my own life flinging.
It cannot be: my heart is rent too deep;
And from the wounds I feel all freely flowing
My hot life's-blood. I faint in earth's damp meadows;
'Tis dark,—and darker,—as in nightmare-trances,
And silent shuddering I cast my glances
To the far realm of Clouds, where quiet shadows
Their soft dim arms with love are round me throwing.

PROLOGUE.

Es war 'mal ein Ritter, trübselig und stumm.

THERE once was a knight, sad and silent was he,
With pale cheeks, and eyeballs deep buried,
Who went awkwardly stumbling with tottering knee,
In dreams or in brown studies buried.
So wooden, so clumsy, of grace all bereft,
The flowers and the maidens all laughed right and left
When past them he blundering hurried.

Oft he sat in the gloomiest corner at home,
Before men he was silent and fluttered,
And yearned with stretched arms, as for some one to come,
Yet scarcely a syllable muttered:
But when midnight had fallen o'er the sorrowful man,
A strange musical ringing and singing began,
And a tapping with whispering soft uttered.

And in gently gliding his love met his sight,
  In soft rustling foam-garments gleaming,
Blowing and glowing like rose-leaves in light,
  Her veil with fair star-jewels beaming;
Gold ringlets at will round her slender form play,
Her eyes greet his own, and he owns their sweet sway:
  They embrace,—he no longer is dreaming.

With love-might he holds her, his fears are all fled,
  Right bravely the Dull One is glowing;
The Dreamer awakes, and the Pale One is red,
  And the Timid a bold one is growing.
But now by his love he is roguishly mocked;
His head she has covered and merrily locked
  With her diamond-starred, white veil long flowing.

In a crystalline palace, deep under the sea,
  The good knight enchanted is straying;
He stares in wild wonder, and scarcely can see,
  For the splendor and glory bright raying.
But the Nixie in love holds him fast to her side,
The knight is a bridegroom, the Nixie is bride,
  And her maidens the cithern are playing.

They're playing and singing, and singing so well,
  Ah! who in that wild dance is fleetest?
The knight is half giddy, his heart seems to swell,
  And more firmly he clings to the Sweetest,
When sudden a darkness o'er all seems to come,
And the good knight again sits so lonely at home
  In his close little poet's chamber!

1.

Im wunderschönen Monat Mai.

IN the wondrous lovely month of May,
  When all the buds were blowing,
All in my heart one morning
  I felt that Love was flowing.

All in the loveliest month, in May,
  When bird-pipes all were going,
I went to her, confessing
  The deep love in me growing.

2.

Aus meinen Thränen sprießen
Viel blühende Blumen hervor.

UP from my tears are growing
  Fair flowers in many vales,
And from my sighs go flying
  A choir of nightingales.

And if thou dost love me, darling,
  I will give thee all the flowers,
And the nightingales at thy window
  Shall sing through summer hours.

3.

Die Rose, die Lilie, die Taube, die Sonne.

FOR the dove or the sun, rose or lily sweet growing,
  For all in love's rapture I once was deep glowing;

Thou lov'st them no more,—for her only thou carest,
The rarest, the fairest, the purest, the dearest;
She only, fount of all love flowing,
Is the dove and the sun, rose and lily sweet growing.

4.

Wenn ich in Deine Augen seh'.

WHENE'ER into thine eyes I see,
All pain and sorrow fly from me;
But when again I kiss thy mouth,
Then I am strong and full of youth.

And when I lean upon thy breast,
The joys of heaven in me rest;
But when thou sayest, "I love thee!"
Then I must weep, and bitterly.

5.

Dein Angesicht so lieb und schön.

THAT face which ever fair did seem
I saw but lately in a dream,
Sweet as if clad in angel's veil,
And yet so pale, so sadly pale.

Thy lips alone are red to-night;
But Death ere long must kiss them white,
And quenched will be the rays divine
Which in thy gentle glances shine.

6.

Lehn' Deine Wang' an meine Wang'.

OH, lay thy cheek against my cheek,
 Let the tears in one stream go flowing;
And to my heart press firm thy heart,
 Let the flames be together glowing!

And when the stream of our tears shall have flown
 On that wild fire hotly burning,
And when my arms round thee are thrown,
 I shall die for pure love-yearning.

7.

Ich will meine Seele tauchen.

I WILL pour all my soul's deep feeling
 In the cup of the lily, like wine;
And the lily shall breathe, soft pealing,
 A lay of the loved one mine.

The song shall go trembling and thrilling
 With all that kiss's power,
The kiss which she gave so willing
 In the tenderest, sweetest hour.

8.

Es stehen unbeweglich
 Die Sterne in der Höh',
Viel Tausend Jahr', und schauen
 Sich an mit Liebesweh.

THE stars have stood unmoving
 Thousands of years above,

Each gazing on the other
 In the fond pain of love.

They speak a copious language,
 The sweetest ever heard;
Yet none of all the linguists
 Can speak of it a word.

Yet I right well have learned it,
 Through every tense and case;
And the grammar of my study
 Was my heart's own dearest's face.

9.

Auf Flügeln des Gesanges.

ON the wings of song far sweeping,
 Heart's dearest, with me thou'lt go
Away where the Ganges is creeping:
 Its loveliest garden I know,—

A garden where roses are burning
 In the moonlight all silent there;
Where the lotus-flowers are yearning
 For their sister beloved and fair.

The violets titter, caressing,
 Peeping up as the planets appear,
And the roses, their warm love confessing,
 Whisper words, soft-perfumed, to each ear.

And, gracefully lurking or leaping,
 The gentle gazelles come round;

While afar, deep rushing and sweeping,
The waves of the Ganges sound.

We'll lie there, in slumber sinking
'Neath the palm-trees by the stream,
Rapture and rest deep drinking,
Dreaming the happiest dream.

10.

Die Lotosblume ängstigt
Sich vor die Sonne Pracht,
Und mit gesenktem Haupte
Erwartet sie die Nacht.

THE lotus-blossom suffers
In the sun's splendid light;
And, with her head declining,
She is waiting for the night.

The moon is her own lover;
He wakes her with his rays,
And, her flower-face unveiling,
She sweetly meets his gaze.

She glows and blows, white-beaming,
Looks silent on high again,
Perfuming and weeping and trembling
In love and love's sweet pain.*

---

* She blooms, and glows, and glistens,
And gazes calmly above;
She sighs, and weeps, and trembles
From love and the pain of love.
Translated by "H. K."

11.

Im Rhein, im schönen Strome.

IN the Rhine, in the glorious river,
  Reflected as waves roll on,
With its high cathedral ever,
  Lies the holy, great Cologne.

In that church a picture o'er me
  Hangs, on golden leather traced:
Often it has shone before me
  Like a light in life's dark waste.

Angels and flowers tremble
  In joy round our Lady above;
Her eyes, lips, and cheeks resemble
  Exactly the face of my love.

12.

Du liebst mich nicht, Du liebst mich nicht.

YOU love me not, you love me not;
  With that I'm not tormented;
For I am happy every jot
  On you to gaze contented.

You hate me, oh, you're hating me;
  Such is your red mouth's story:
Oh, hold it out to kisses free,
  And I shall pant in glory.

13.

Du sollst mich liebend umschliessen
Geliebtes, schönes Weib.

COME, twine in wild rapture round me,
  Fair woman beloved and warm,
Till thy feet and arms have bound me
  And I'm wreathed with thy supple form!

* * * * *

She has twined with strength enraptured,
  Her folds are all round me thrown;
And the fairest of snakes has captured
  The happiest Laocöon.

14.

O schwöre nicht, und küsse nur.

OH, do not vow, but only kiss,
  For I no woman's oath believe!
Thy words are sweet, but sweeter is
  The kiss which I from thee receive!
For that I have, in that I've faith;
All words are idle mist and breath.

* * * * *

Oh, swear, my dearest,—for I think
  All true while panting on thy breast!
When raptured in its charms I sink,
  I *do* believe—that I am blest;
Believe that all eternally,
And longer still, thou'lt love but me!

15.

Auf meiner Herzliebsten Aeugelein.

UPON my darling's lovely eyes
  Sweet canzonets I've written,
And on that mouth I dearly prize
  The best of *terze rime*,
And on those cheeks where rose-bloom lies
  A brave array of stanzas;
And had she a heart as well as a head,
Long ago a sonnet I on it had made.

16.

Die Welt ist dumm, die Welt ist blind.

THE world's a fool, the world is blind,
  And grows simple to aggravation:
It says of thee, dear—nay, never mind!—
  Thou hast lost thy reputation!

The world is stupid, the world is blind,
  And justice it never will do thee:
It knows not how sweet are thy kisses kind,
  Or how rapture goes quivering through thee.

17.

Liebste, sollst mir heute sagen:
  Bist Du nicht ein Traumgebild',
Wie's in schwülen Sommertagen
  Aus dem Hirn des Dichter's quillt?

DREAMY phantoms, fair and fleeting,
  From the poet's brain oft run

When the summer days are heating:—
Dearest, art thou such a one?

And—yet no. A mouth so smiling,
Eyes where such a magic played,
Such a dainty thing, beguiling
Poet never yet hath made.

Vampires, basilisks, and terrors,
Dragons which by lindens crawl,
Monsters bred of lies and errors,
Poets truly made them all.

But that mouth where mischief dances,
And thyself, and winning face,
And thy treacherous gentle glances,—
Poet never dreamed such grace.

18.

Wie die Wellenschaumgeborene.

LIKE the foam-born of the waters,
Gleams my love in beauty's pride;
But that fairest of earth's daughters
Is a stranger's chosen bride.

Heart, keep patience; never lose it;
Murmur not that thou'rt betrayed;
Bear it, bear it, and excuse it
To the lovely, stupid maid.

19.

Ich grolle nicht, und wenn das Herz auch bricht.

I *WILL* be patient, though my heart should break,
  Thou love forever lost! no plaint I'll make.
But though thou glitterest in diamonds bright,
There falls no gleam into thy heart's deep night.

I saw't in dreams, I knew it long ago;
I saw the night through thy heart's chambers flow;
I saw the snake which gnaws upon thy heart;
I saw, my love, how wretched still thou art.

20.

Ja, Du bist elend, und ich grolle nicht.

YES, thou art wretched, but I'll not complain;—
  My love, together we will wretched be!
Until death breaks the heart long sick with pain,
  My love, together we will wretched be!

I see the scorn which oft thy lip repeats,
  I see defiance flashing from thine eye,
I see the pride which in thy bosom beats:—
  Yet thou art wretched, wretched e'en as I.

Thy lips show agonies unseen around,
  And hidden tears in those bright eyes I see;
Thy haughty bosom hides a secret wound:
  My love, my love, we both will wretched be!

21.

Das ist ein Flöten und Geigen.

VIOL and flute are sounding,
And trumpet-tones entwine;
And in the bride-dance bounding
Goes that heart's love of mine.

There is a ringing and groaning
Of drums and trumpets deep;
Between there's a sobbing and moaning
Of angels who sorrowing weep.

22.

So hast Du ganz und gar vergessen.

SO you have forgotten altogether
That I held your heart so long in tether,—
Your heart so sweet and so false and so wee?
A sweeter and falser one nowhere can be.

And I ask of the love and long suffering whether
You think how they pressed my heart together;
I know not if love were greater than woe,
But that both were too great for me well do I know!

23.

Und wüßten's die Blumen, die kleinen.

AND if the small flowers but knew it,
How deep are the wounds of my heart,
Weeping with me they would rue it,
To heal all my pain and smart.

And had the nightingales feeling
  Of my weariness and grief,
Their songs would come gayly pealing
  To give my pain relief.

And if the stars in heaven
  My sufferings could know,
Their light would soon be given
  To mitigate my woe.

But none of them can know it;
  One only knows my pain;
And she who alone could do it
  Has rent my heart in twain.

24.

Warum sind denn die Rosen so blaß?

WHY are the roses so pale of hue,
    Oh, tell me, dearest, why?
Why in the grass fresh bathed in dew
  Do the violets silent lie?

Why does the lark far-sailing fleet
  Sing with such wailing cries?
And why from the sweet meadow-sweet
  Do corpse-like vapors rise?

And why does the sun on the meadow gleam
  With such a chilling gloom?
Why is the earth so gray and grim,
  And dismal as a tomb?

Why am I myself so sad and lone,
  My dearest darling, say?
Oh, speak, my heart's all-dearest one,
  Why did you turn away?

25.

Sie haben Dir viel erzählet,
Und haben viel geklagt.

O'ER me they much lamented,
  Of me harsh tales you've heard;
But of what my soul tormented
  They never spoke a word.

Their outcry was most uncivil;
  They shook their heads o'er my fall;
They called me the very devil,
  And you believed it all!

But what should have been the first thing
  Not one of them e'er guessed;
The stupidest, worst, and curst thing
  I secretly hid in my breast.

26.

Die Linde blühte, die Nachtigall sang.

THE lindens blossomed, the nightingale sung,
  The sun like a true friend smiled with the rest;
You gave me a kiss, and your arm round me flung,
  And pressed me right close to your dear heaving
    breast.

The dead leaves were flying, the raven's croak fell,
  The sun peeped out grim as if bent to displease;
Then we gave to each other a frosty "farewell!"
  And you courteously courtsied the gracefullest "cheese."*

27.

Wir haben viel für einander gefühlt.

WE'VE had many a sympathetic thought,
  Without ever once from propriety straying;
We never have quarrelled and never fought,
  Though "husband and wife" we once oft were playing.
We have played together with merry jest,
And tenderly kissed in embraces pressed,
  Until we at last, in childish fun,
Played at hide-and-seek in wood and by river;
  And, ah! our hiding so well was done
That we've hidden ourselves from each other forever.

28.

Du bliebest mir treu am längsten.

TO me thou wert true the longest,
  For me thou hast interceded;
  Thou gav'st me comfort when needed,
When pain and need were strongest.

* Da knixtest Du höflich den höflichsten Knix.

Food and drink thou hast brought me,
  Thy money thou didst lend me,
  My linen thou didst mend me,
And my travelling passport got me.

God guard her I loved so blindly
  From cold and from heat forever!
  And may he punish her never
For treating me so kindly!

29.

Die Erde war so lange geizig,
  Da kam der Mai, und sie ward spendabel,
Und Alles lacht und jauchzt, und freut sich,
  Ich aber bin nicht zum Lachen capabel.

TOO long had the earth kept back its treasure;
  At last May came with her riches spendible,
And all things laughed and beamed with pleasure:
  I only remained of all unbendable.

Flowers were sprouting, and May-bells ringing,
  The birds, in fact, seemed quite comprehendible;
But I found no joy in their chat or singing,
  And I only wished it were all suspendible.

Every one bored me with bow or salaam,
  They wondered to find me so very offendable,—
All because my love is now styled *Madame;*
  And the matter, I fear, is not amendable.

30.

Und als ich so lange, so lange gesäumt.

AND as I so long, oh, so long delayed,
When in distant lands I dreaming strayed,
To wait, to my darling seemed distress:
So she sewed for herself a wedding-dress,
Till she finally held in her tender embraces
The dullest of fools whom dulness disgraces.

My darling is so sweet and mild,
She is ever before me,—the gentle child;
Her violet eyes and her rose-tinted skin,
Glowing and blowing year out, year in.
That I from such a love went straying,
Was the stupidest trick I was e'er caught playing.

31.

Die blauen Veilchen der Aeugelein.

O'ER violets blue her eyelids fall,
Ruddy roses her cheeks we call,
Snow-white lilies her hands so small,
Which bloom and bloom and never fade:
Only the little heart is dead.

32.

Die Welt ist so schön und der Himmel so blau.

THE world is so fair, and the heaven so blue,
And the breezes blowing so softly woo,

And the flowers on the meadow come blooming anew,
Glittering and gleaming in morning dew,
And I see men rejoicing at every view;
And yet I would fain in my grave be sleeping,
By a dead love lying, up to her creeping.

33.

Mein süßes Lieb, wenn Du im Grab'.

MY own dear love, when in the tomb—
The gloomy tomb—you're sleeping,
Then I unto your side will come,
Up to you softly creeping.

I'll press you, caress you with kisses wild,
My cold, silent, pale one, with yearning,
Rejoicing and trembling and weeping till wild,
Until I to a white corpse am turning.

The dead may arise when midnight calls,
In aerial dances flying;
But we will keep still 'neath the tomb's close walls,
Embracing and silently lying.

The dead will arise on the Judgment Day,
To be saved, or from heaven to sever:
We will give it no thought,—we'll have nothing to say,
But will slumber and slumber forever.

34.

Ein Fichtenbaum steht einsam.

A PINE-TREE'S standing lonely
  In the North on a mountain's brow,
Nodding, with whitest cover,
  Wrapped up by the ice and snow.

He's dreaming of a palm-tree,
  Which, far in the Morning Land,
Lonely and silent sorrows
  Mid burning rocks and sand.*

35.

Schöne, helle, goldne Sterne.

LOVELY, gleaming, golden star,
  Greet my darling when afar!
Say I'm always, since we part,
Pale and true and sick at heart.

---

* Few poems surpass this either in beauty and simplicity of form or depth of expression. That it was one of Heine's own favorites may be inferred from his having placed a part of it as motto to "The New Spring" in his "Pictures of Travel." The original is as follows:—

Ein Fichtenbaum steht einsam
  Im Norden auf kahler Höh'.
Ihn schläfert; mit weißer Decke
  Umhüllen ihn Eis und Schnee.

Er träumt von einer Palme,
  Die, fern im Morgenland,
Einsam und schweigend trauert
  Auf brennender Felsenwand.

36.

Ach, wenn ich nur der Schemel wär'.

The Head speaks.

AH! could I but the footstool be
On which my darling rests her feet!
Although right hard she stamped on me,
I would not murmur when they beat.

The Heart speaks.

Ah! if I might the cushion be
Which she oft sticks her needles in!
However she might torture me,
I would not mind the pricks a pin.

The Song speaks.

Could I the piece of paper be
Which she around a ringlet wreathes!
Into her ear I'd whisper free
The love which in me lives and breathes.

37.

Seit die Liebste war entfernt.

SINCE my sweetheart went away,
I've forgotten to be gay;
Many a jester made his joke,
But I neither laughed nor spoke.

Since her love no more I keep,
I have also ceased to weep;
Though with woe my heart nigh breaks,
Every tear my eye forsakes.

38.

Aus meinen großen Schmerzen.

FROM the great pain of my spirit
Come the little songs I am singing,
Which, in music their flight upwinging,
To her cold heart fluttering bear it.

They fly to my love from her lover,
Then return to me moaning and crying,
Yet will not tell with their sighing
What it is in her heart they discover.

39.

Ich kann es nicht vergessen.

TOO oft I cannot bless thee,
Thou loved and loveliest one,
That I did once possess thee,
Body and soul mine own.

And, oh, but I would be merry
If the body so sweet I might woo!
The soul ye might take and bury:
I have soul enough for two.

I will cut my soul asunder,
And breathe in a half to thee,
And twine myself round thee so tender,—
One body, one soul we will be.

40.

Philister in Sonntagsröcklein.

TOWN-SNOBBIES, their Sunday keeping,
  Go walking through wood and plain,
Rejoicing, while kid-like they're leaping,
  To gaze on "fair Nature" again.

They stare with dull eyes gazing
  At all the romantic show,
And their long ears deem amazing
  The sparrows, as on they go.

But I carefully draw my curtain,
  And with black I hang my wall;
E'en to-day my ghosts, I'm certain,
  Will pay me a morning call.

The old love comes gently sweeping
  Afar from the land of death;
She sits herself by me, weeping,
  And my heart grows soft in her breath.

41.

Manch Bild vergessener Zeiten.

THE forms of times forgotten
  Oft from their graves revive,
And show me how when near thee
  I once was wont to live.

By day through the streets I wandered,
  And, as I wandered, dreamed;
All gazed on me and marvelled,
  So sad and mute I seemed.

In the night-time it was better:
  Then the streets were silent ground;
I and my shadow together,
  We wandered silent around,—

Wandered with echoing footstep
  Over the bridge and brook;
The moon through clouds came breaking,
  And greeted with solemn look.

I stood before thy dwelling,
  I looked the windows o'er;
I looked upon thy window,
  And, oh! but my heart was sore!

I know thou'st looked from the window
  Full often on the square,
And seen me in the moonlight
  Stand like a pillar there.

42.

Ein Jüngling liebt ein Mädchen.

A YOUNG man loves a maiden
  Who another youth prefers;
The other, he loved another,
  And has joined his fate to hers.

The maiden marries from anger,
  Accepting the very next
Who comes in the way with an offer,
  And the youth is sorely vexed.

It is an old, old story,
  And yet 'tis ever new;
And he to whom it answers,
  It breaks his heart in two.

43.

Freundschaft, Liebe, Stein der Weisen.

THE Elixir Vitæ, friendship, love!
  Oft their praise my soul would move,
And I praised and sought each one,
But of all discovered none.

44.

Hör' ich das Liedchen klingen.

HEAR I the ballad ringing
  Which once my loved one sang:
My heart in twain seems springing,
  So wildly shoots the pang.

I am driven by gloomy yearning
  Far up to the forest gray;
And there, into hot tears turning,
  My sorrow goes flowing away.

45.

Mir träumte von einem Königskind.

I DREAMED of the fairest princess seen,
  With the palest of tearful faces;
We sat all under the linden green,
  Held fast in love's embraces.

"I do not wish thy father's throne,
  Nor his sceptre of gold, O dearest,
Nor do I seek his diamond crown,
  But thou, and thou only, O fairest!"

"That may not be," said she to me;
  "I was laid in my grave too early;
And only by night I come to thee,
  Because I love thee so dearly."

46.

Mein Liebchen wir saßen beisammen.

MY love, in our light boat riding,
  We sat at the close of day,
And still through the night went gliding
  Afar on our watery way.

The Spirit-Isle, soft glowing,
  Lay dimmering 'neath moon and star;
There music was softly flowing,
  And cloud-dances waved afar,

And ever more sweetly pealing,
  And waving more winningly;
But past it our boat went stealing
  All sad on the wide, wide sea.

47.

Aus alten Mährchen winkt es.

FROM ancient legends springing,
  Beckons a snowy hand,
With a ringing and a singing,
  And all of a magic land,

Where strange large flowers are yearning
  In golden eventides,
All passionately burning,
  Gazing like longing brides;

Where all the trees are speaking,
  And singing like a choir,
And fountains pure fall breaking
  In music on the air,—

Love's sweetest airs prolonging,
  Such as thou ne'er didst know,
Until strange love and longing
  O'er all the spirits flow.

And oh that I were yonder!
  How blest my heart would be
In that sweet land of wonder,
  How happy and how free!

O Land of Joy!—before me
I see thee oft in dreams!
But when the day dawns o'er me,
It flits like foam on streams.

48.

Ich hab' Dich geliebet, und liebe Dich noch.

I HAVE loved thee long, and I love thee now;
And, though the world should perish,
O'er its dying embers still would glow
The flames of the love I cherish.

* * * * *

And I will love till life be past,
Till death's dark hour is nearing,
Into the eternal grave at last
My life's great love-wound bearing.

49.

Am leuchtenden Sommermorgen.

ON a fair gleaming summer morning
I walk in the garden below;
The flowers are whispering and talking,
But silent among them I go.

The flowers are whispering and talking;
With pity my features they scan:
"Oh, do not be cross to our sister,
Thou sorrowful pale-faced man."

50.

Es leuchtet meine Liebe.

IN the dark garb she's wearing,
  My love herself seems bright,
As when sad tales we're hearing,
  But told in a summer's night:

"In magic garden straying
  Two lovers go mute and lone;
The nightingales are playing,
  In the light of the summer moon.

"The maid scarce speaks or glances;
  Before her kneels the knight;
The Desert Giant advances,
  The lady takes to flight.

"The knight lies bleeding and dying,
  His way the giant doth wend;"—
When I in my grave am lying,
  The tale will have reached its end.

51.

Sie haben mich gequälet.

THEY tortured me completely,
  Goading at fearful rate,
Some with the love they bore me,
  And others with their hate.

In my glass they poured their poison,—
  Yes, poisoned the bread I ate,—
Some with the love they bore me,
  And others with their hate.

But she who mostly tortured
  With sorrow my whole soul moved:
By her I was never hated,
  By her I was never loved.*

52.

Es liegt der heiße Sommer.

THE ruddy rays of summer
  Upon thy cheeks now fall;
But, oh! the frosts of winter
  Are in thy heart so small.

---

* This poem was subsequently parodied by HEINE himself, as follows :—

They *ennuyéed* me sadly,
  And bored me, as you may see,
Some of them with their prose,
  And some with their poesy.

They shocked my ears most sadly,
  In endless disharmony,
Some of them with their prose,
  And some with their poesy.

But those who with their scribbling
  Tried me the most the while
Wrote neither in good poetic
  Nor in good prosaic style.

Some day there'll be a change, love,
A change in every part!
The winter 'll be on the cheeks, love,
The summer in your heart.

53.

Wann zwei von einander scheiden.

OFTEN when two are parting,
Each grasps a hand as friend;
And then begins a weeping
And a sighing without end.

We did not sigh when parting;
No tears between us fell;
The weeping and the sighing
Came after our farewell.

54.

Sie saßen und tranken am Theetisch.

WITH feelings refined and poetic,
They talked, o'er their teacups, of love:
The gentlemen all were æsthetic,
The ladies, all easy to move.

"Our love should all be platonic,"
The dry old Hofrath cried;
His lusty dame's smile was ironic,
And yet from her heart she sighed.

Like an oracle spoke the parson :—
"If in love too far we go,
It is bad for the constitution."
Young lady lisped out, "Why so?"

"Love!—ah, love is a passion,"
Said the countess, in tenderest tone,
And gave, in her tenderest fashion,
A cup to the Herr Barōn.

There was still a place at the table:
You should have been there, my dove,
To give us, as well as you're able,
Your experience in love.

55.

Vergiftet sind meine Lieder,
Wie könnt' es anders sein?

MY songs are full of poison :—
How could it different be?
Since thou'st been pouring poison
O'er the bloom of life for me.

My songs are full of poison ;—
And poisoned they well may be:
I bear in my heart many serpents,
And with them, beloved, thee.

56.

Mir träumte wieder der alte Traum.

THE dream of old came over me:
'Twas May night by the river:
We sat beneath the linden-tree
And swore to be true forever.

A swearing by one, a swearing by both,
Kissing, cooing, and all, to delight me;
And, to make me remember thy joy and my oath,
In thy rapture thou deeply didst bite me.

Oh, biting love with eyes of light!
Why pass all rules unheeded?
To swear was regular and right,
The biting was not needed.

57.

Ich steh' auf des Berges Spitze,
Und werde sentimental.

I STAND upon a mountain,
Singing sentimental rhymes.
"Oh that I were a birdling!"
I sigh a thousand times.

And if I were a swallow,
I'd fly, my child, to thee;
And were thy windows open,
Oh, there my nest should be.

And if I were a nightingale,
By thee I'd still be seen,
And sing by night my songs of love
All on the linden green.

Or if I were a mocking-bird,
Unto thy heart I'd flee;
Thou lovest well all mocking-birds,
Or aught like mockery.*

58.

Mein Wagen rollet langsam.

MY coach goes slowly rolling
All through the greenwood gay,
Through flowery dales enchanting,
Which bloom in the sunny ray.

Of my lady-love musing and dreaming,
I sit, when three forms approach,
Three shadowy forms, which, greeting
And nodding, peer into the coach.

They leap and make grimaces,
So mocking, and yet so shy,
And whirl up like mists together,
And, tittering, go darting by.

---

* Wenn ich ein Gimpel wäre,
So flög' ich gleich an Dein Herz;
Du bist ja hold den Gimpeln,
Und heilest Gimpelschmerz.

GIMPEL, a bulfinch, a dolt or simpleton.

59.

Ich hab' im Traum geweinet.

I WEPT while I was dreaming
  That thou didst buried lie;
I woke, and with my weeping
  My cheeks were not yet dry.

I wept while I was dreaming
  That thou hadst gone from me;
I woke, and still kept weeping
  Full long and bitterly.

I wept while I was dreaming
  That thou didst love me well;
I woke, and—woe is me, love!—
  My tears are flowing still.

60.

Allnächtlich im Traume seh' ich Dich.*

EACH night in dreams thou com'st to me,
  I hear thee gently calling,
And then, loud weeping, leap to thee,
  At thy dear feet down falling.

---

* Of this poem FRIEDRICH STEINMANN tells us, in his work on HEINE (*Denkwürdigkeiten und Erlebnisse*, Leipzig, 1857), that when first read in Berlin by the author before the literary circle of the VON ENSES, CHAMISSO, GANS, HELMINE VON CHÉZY, and

Thou look'st on me so mournfully,
  Thy fair blonde tresses shaking;
Then from thine eyes all tremblingly
  The pearly tears come breaking.

Thou breathest a word in under-tone,
  And givest me cypress braided:
I wake,—and the cypress-wreath is gone,
  And the word from my memory faded.

61.

Das ist ein Brausen und Heulen.

THE wind and the rain are playing,
  And the autumn storm roars wild:
Oh, where may she be straying,
  My poor unhappy child?

At her window sadly dreaming,
  In her little, lonely room,
Her eyes with tear-drops gleaming,
  She looks out into gloom.

62.

Der Herbstwind rüttelt die Bäume.

THE Fall-wind rattles the branches,
  The night is chilly grown,

---

others who were wont to assemble at the house of ELISE VON HOHENHAUSEN, it excited so much merry opposition—in other words, was so good-naturedly laughed at—that it was at the time withheld from publication.

And, wrapped in my dark-gray mantle,
  I ride through the wood alone.

And as I ride, so riding
  My thoughts go on before;
They carry me, light and lively,
  Up to my true love's door.

The hounds bay loud, and the servants
  Their flaring torches bring;
I rush up the winding staircase,
  My steel spurs rattle and ring.

In her well-lighted tapestried chamber,
  Where all is sweet-perfumed and warm,
The beautiful darling awaits me;
  And at last we are fast arm in arm.

The oak-tree speaks in the forest,
  Where the leaves on the storm-wind stream:
"What wilt thou, O foolish rider,
  With this thy foolish dream?"

63.

Es fällt ein Stern herunter.

YONDER a star is falling
  From its far-gleaming height:
That is the star of love, alone:
  I see its fading light!

Blossoms and leaves are falling
  From the apple-tree to the ground,
And the merry mocking breezes
  Come driving them round and round.

The swan on the lake is singing,
  While up and down he rows;
And with softer song and softer
  To his watery grave he goes.

And all is dark and silent:
  On the wind fly leaf and flower;
The star is scattered in ashes,
  And the song of the swan is o'er.

64.

Der Traumgott bracht' mich in ein Riesenschloß.

THE Dream-God brought me to a giant pile,
  Mid sweet enchanted scents and tapers burning,
Where a strange, motley throng pressed on the while,
  Through labyrinthine chambers strangely turning.
The pale crowd seeking exit filled each aisle,
  Wringing their hands and wailing in wild yearning.
Maidens and knights I marked among the many;
And I am hurled along as swift as any.

When suddenly I'm all alone, and so
  I stare that naught remains of crowd reminding,
Then wander on alone, and haste and go
  Through all the chambers marvellously winding.

My feet seem lead, my heart all fright and woe,
And now I deem the exit past all finding.
At length, however, to the gate I fare,
And now I go——Oh, God! who's standing there?

I saw my love upon that threshold stand,
Her brow all bent with care, her lips with sorrow.
I should return, she showed it with her hand:
Was it a threat or warning for the morrow?
A sweet fire from her eyes flashed forth command,
Till heart and brain seemed a new strength to borrow;
Strange, lovely, stern, the thoughts those glances spoke,
And yet so full of love! With that I woke.

65.

Die Mitternacht war kalt und stumm.

THE midnight air was cold and rude,
I wandered wailing through the wood;
But though the trees from their sleep I waken,
Above me in pity their heads are shaken.

66.

Am Kreuzweg wird begraben.

THE suicide lies buried
Where the cross-roads pass o'er;
There a blue flower is growing,
Called The Poor Sinner's Flower.

I stood on the cross-road, sighing,
  In the cold midnight hour;
Slowly in moonlight waving
  I saw The Poor Sinner's Flower.

67.

Wo ich bin, mich rings umdunkelt.

WHERE I am, still darker o'er me
  Deeper darkness seems to rise,
Since no longer flash before me,
  Dearest love, thy lovely eyes.

Clouded is the heavenly dawning
  Of my love-star's golden light;
At my feet the abyss is yawning ·
  Take me, ancient, endless Night!

68.

Nacht lag auf meinen Augen.

NIGHT lay upon my eyelids,
  Lead lay upon my mouth;
With brain and heart all frozen
  I lay in the grave of youth.

I cannot tell how long it was
  I slumbered in the cave,
Till I awoke and listened
  To a knocking in my grave.

"Will you not rise, my Henry?
  The Judgment-Day comes on,

And all the Dead are risen,
  Their endless joy begun."

"Dear love, there is no rising
  For one forever blind:
The sight I lost through weeping
  I never again shall find."

"But from your eyes, my Henry,
  I'll kiss the night away;
And you shall see the angels
  And Heaven's glorious day."

"I cannot rise, my darling:
  It bleeds, as from a sword,
Where in my heart you stabbed me
  With one sharp-pointed word."

"But very gently, Henry,
  I'll press your heart again,
And that will stanch the bleeding,
  And that will heal the pain."

"I cannot rise, my darling:
  My head is bleeding, see,
Where long ago I fired the shot
  When you were stolen from me!"

"But with my tresses, Henry,
  Your head may well be bound;
And that will stop the bleeding
  And cure the cruel wound."

She prayed so softly, sweetly,
  I could not say her no:
So with the one I loved so well
  I sought to rise and go.

Then all my wounds burst open,
  And like a torrent broke
From head and heart the blood-stream;
  And then—in haste I woke.

69.

Die alten, bösen Lieder.

THE old and evil ballads,
  The dreams with bitter sting,—
Come now and let us bury them:
  So, a great coffin bring!

I have much to lay within it;
  But *what* mayn't yet be known,
Or why the coffin is greater
  Than the Heidelberger Tun.

And bring me a death-bier with it,
  Of planks both thick and strong;
For it must be much longer
  Than the bridge of Mainz is long.

Then bring twelve giants, stronger
  Than Christopher whose shrine
Is in Cologne cathedral
  Beside the rolling Rhine.

And they shall carry the coffin
  And sink it in the sea ;
For to such a mighty coffin
  A mighty grave should be.

Do you know why the coffin
  So heavy and great must be?
Because in it I laid my love,
  And with it my miscry.

Trivial half-way joys we hate,
  Hate all childish fancies.
If no crime weigh down the soul,
Why should we endure control
  And groan in death-like trances?
The puling wight looks down and sighs,
But the brave man lifts his eyes
  Up to Heaven's bright glances.

IMMERMANN.

1.

In mein gar zu dunkles Leben.

IN my life too dark and dreary
  Once gleamed an image bright:
That lovely form is faded,
  And I am wrapped in night.

When children stray in darkness,
  And fears around them throng,
To drive away their terror
  They sing aloud a song.

Thus like a child I'm singing
As life's dark shades draw near;
And though my lay lack music,
It drives away my fear.

2.

Ich weiß nicht, was soll es bedeuten.

I KNOW not what sorrow is o'er me,
What spell is upon my heart;
But a tale of old times is before me,—
A legend that will not depart.

Night falls as I linger, dreaming,
And calmly flows the Rhine;
The peaks of the hills are gleaming
In the golden sunset-shine.

A wondrous lovely maiden
Sits high in glory there;
Her robe with gems is laden,
And she combs her golden hair.

And she spreads out the golden treasure,
Still singing in harmony;
And the song has a mystical measure
And a wonderful melody.

The boatman, when once she has bound him,
Is lost in a wild sad love;
He sees not the rocks around him,
He sees but the beauty above.

I believe that the billows springing
  The boat and the boatman drown;
And all that with her magical singing
  The Loré-lay has done.

3.

Mein Herz, mein Herz ist traurig.

MY heart, my heart is weary,
  Yet merrily beams the May;
And I lean against the linden,
  High up on the terrace gray.

The town-moat far below me
  Runs silent, and sad, and blue:
A boy in a boat floats o'er it,
  Still fishing and whistling too.

And a beautiful varied picture
  Spreads out beyond the flood,—
Fair houses, and gardens, and people,
  And cattle, and meadow, and wood.

Young maidens are bleaching the linen,
  They leap as they go and come;
And the mill-wheel is dripping with diamonds,
  I list to its far-away hum.

And high on yon old gray castle
  A sentry-box peeps o'er;
While a young red-coated soldier
  Is pacing beside the door.

He handles his shining musket,
  Which gleams in the sunlight red;
He halts, he presents, and shoulders:—
  I wish that he'd shoot me dead!

4.

Im Walde wandl' ich und weine.

IN the woods I wander weeping:
  The thrush sits on the spray;
She springs and sings, while peeping,
  Oh, why so sad to-day?

Your sister, dear, the swallow,
  Quite well the reason knows;
She builds her nest, she'll follow
  My sweetheart where she goes.

5.

Die Nacht ist feucht und stürmisch.

THE night is wet and stormy,
  The heaven black above;
In the wood beneath rustling branches
  All silently I rove.

From the lonely hunter's cottage
  A light beams cheerily;
But it will not tempt me thither,
  Where all is sad to see.

The blind old grandmother's sitting
  Alone in the leathern chair,

Uncanny and stern as an image,
  And speaking to no one there.

The red-headed son of the hunter
  Walks cursing up and down,
And casts in a corner his rifle,
  With a bitter laugh and a frown.

A maiden is spinning and weeping,
  And moistens the flax with tears;
While at her small feet, whimpering,
  Lies a hound with drooping ears.

6.

Als ich auf der Reise, zufällig.

AS I once by chance on a journey
  My lady-love's family found,
Little sister, and father, and mother,
  Came joyfully greeting around.

They asked, of course, "How I found me?"
  Hoping my health would not fail;
For, although quite the same as ever,
  My countenance seemed to be pale.

I asked of the aunts and the cousins,
  Of many bores whom we know,
And then of the little greyhound
  With his bark so soft and low.

Of the loved one—long since married—
  Then I asked, by the way,—though late;

And her father, smiling, whispered
  Of her "interesting state."

And I gave my congratulations
  On the delicate event,
And to her and to all relations
  "Best remembrances" were sent.

But the little sister shouted,
  That the dog which once was mine
Had gone mad in early summer:
  "So we drowned him in the Rhine."

That child is so like her sister,—
  Especially when they smile:
She has the same soft glances
  Which tortured me a while.

7.

Wir saßen am Fischerhause.

WE sat by the fisher's cottage
  And looked at the stormy tide;
The evening mist came rising,
  And floating far and wide.

One by one in the light-house
  The lamps shone out on high;
And far on the dim horizon
  A ship went sailing by.

We spoke of storm and shipwreck,
  Of sailors who live on the deep,

And how between sky and water
  And terror and joy they sweep.

We spoke of distant countries,
  In regions strange and fair,
And of the wondrous beings
  And curious customs there;

Of perfumes and lights on the Ganges,
  Where trees like giants tower,
And of beautiful silent beings
  Who kneel to the lotus-flower;

Of the wretched dwarfs of Lapland,
  Broad-headed, wide-mouthed, and small,
Who crouch round their oil-fires, cooking,
  And chatter and scream and bawl.

And the maidens earnestly listened,
  Till at last we spoke no more:
The ship like a shadow had vanished,
  And darkness fell deep on the shore.

8.

Du schönes Fischermädchen,
Treibe den Kahn an's Land.

MY gentle ferry-maiden,
  Come, push the boat to land,
And sit thee down beside me,
  Caressing with hand in hand.

Lay thy head against my bosom,
  And have no fear of me:

Dost thou not venture boldly
  Each day on the roaring sea?

My heart is like the ocean;
  It has storm, and ebb, and flow,
And many a pearl is hidden
  In its silent depths below.

9.

Der Mond ist aufgegangen.

THE moon is high in heaven,
  And shimmers o'er the sea;
And my heart throbs like my dear one's,
  As she silently sits by me.

With my arm around the darling,
  I rest upon the strand:
"What sound is in the night-wind?
  Why trembles your snow-white hand?"

"Those are no evening breezes,
  But the mermaids singing low,—
The mermaids, once my sisters,
  Who were drowned so long ago."

10.

Auf den Wolken ruht der Mond,
Eine Riesenpommeranze.

THE quiet moon upon the clouds
  Like a giant orange is glowing,
While, far beneath, the old gray sea,
  All striped with silver, is flowing.

Alone I wander on the strand,
Where the white surf is broken,
But hear full many a gentle word
Amid the waves soft spoken.

But, oh, the night is far too long;
Silence too long has bound me:
Fair water-fairies, come to me,
And dance and sing around me.

Oh, take my head upon your lap,
Take body and soul in keeping!
But sing me dead,—caress me dead,—
And kiss me to endless sleeping!

11.

Eingehüllt in graue Wolken.

ALL wrapped up in gray cloud-garments,
Now the great gods sleep together;
And I hear their thunder-snoring,
For to-night we've dreadful weather.

Dreadful weather! what a tempest
Threats our ship with dire disaster!
Who will check the mighty storm-wind,
And the waves without a master?

Can't be helped, though, if all nature
A mad holiday *is* keeping:
So I'll wrap me up and slumber,
As the gods above are sleeping.

12.

Der Wind zieht seine Hosen an.

THE wild wind puts his trousers on,—
His foam-white water breeches;
He lashes the waves, and every one
Roars out, and howls, and pitches.

From yon wild height, with furious might,
The rain comes roaring, groaning.
It seems as if the old black Night
The old dark Sea were drowning.

The snow-white sea-gull to our mast
Clings, screaming hoarse, and crying;
And every scream to me doth seem
A deathly prophesying.

13.

Der Sturm spielt auf zum Tanze.

THE wind pipes up for dancing,
The waves in white are clad:
Hurrah!—how the ship is leaping!
And the night is merry and mad.

And living hills of water
Sweep up as the storm-wind calls:
Here a black gulf is gaping,
And there a white tower falls.

And sounds as of sickness and swearing
From the depths of the cabin come:
I keep a firm hold on the bulwarks,
And wish that I now were at home.

14.

Der Abend kommt gezogen.

THE night comes stealing o'er me,
  And clouds are on the sea;
While the wavelets rustle before me
  With a mystical melody.

A water-maid rose singing:
  She sat by me, fair and pale;
And snow-white breasts were springing,
  Like fountains, 'neath her veil.

She kissed me and she pressed me,
  Till I wished her arms away:
"Why hast thou so caressed me,
  Thou lovely Water Fay?"

"Oh, thou need'st not alarm thee
  That thus thy form I hold;
For I only seek to warm me,
  And the night is black and cold."

"The wind to the waves is calling,
  The moonlight is fading away;
And tears down thy cheek are falling,
  Thou beautiful Water Fay!"

"The wind to the waves is calling,
  And the moonlight grows dim on the rocks;
But no tears from mine eyes are falling:
  'Tis the water which drips from my locks."

"The ocean is heaving and sobbing,
The sea-mews scream in the spray;
And thy heart is wildly throbbing,
Thou beautiful Water Fay!"

"My heart is wildly swelling,
And it beats in burning truth;
For I love thee past all telling,
Thou beautiful mortal youth."

15.

Wenn ich an deinem Hause
Des Morgens vorüber geh'.

"WHEN early in the morning
I pass thy window, sweet,
Oh, what a thrill of joy is mine
When both our glances meet!"

"With those dark flashing eyeballs
Which all things round thee scan,
Who art thou, and what seek'st thou,
Thou strange and sickly man?"

"I am a German poet,
Well known in the German land:
Where the first names are written,
Mine own with right may stand.

"And what I seek, my fairest,
Is that for which many pine;
And where men speak of sorrows,
Thou'lt hear them speak of mine."

16.

Das Meer erglänzte weit hinaus.

THE ocean shimmered far around,
  As the last sun-rays shone:
We sat beside the fisher's hut,
  Silent, and all alone.

The mist swam up, the water heaved,
  The sea-mew round us screamed;
And from thy dark eyes, full of love,
  The scalding tear-drops streamed.

I saw them fall upon thy hand;
  Upon my knee I sank,
And from that white and yielding hand
  The glittering tears I drank.

And since that hour I waste away,
  Mid passion's hopes and fears:
O weeping girl!—O weary heart!—
  Thou'rt poisoned with her tears!*

---

* This is the only poem in this volume in which I have departed from the original metre. The following version is in the same metre as the original:—

Far, far away the ocean shone,
  As the last sunbeams fleeted;
Beside the fisher's cabin lone,
  Alone we two were seated.

The mist arose, the water swelled,
  Gulls flew, their flight recalling;

17.

Da droben auf jenem Berge.

HIGH up on yonder mountain
  There stands a lordly hall,
Where dwell three gentle maidens,
  And I was loved by all.

On Saturday Hetty loved me,
  The Sabbath was Julia's day,
And on Monday Kunigunda
  Half squeezed my breath away.

And from thine eyes, which love had filled,
  The tears adown were falling.

I saw them falling on thy hand,
  I on my knee was sinking,
Still as they fell on thy white hand
  Away the tear-drops drinking.

Since that hour my body wastes and wears,
  Yearning to death steals through me;
For that ill-omened woman's tears
  Have been a poison to me.

The reader may remember that a great proportion of words which are monosyllables in English are in two or three syllables in German,—a peculiarity which renders literal translation into the same metre as the original, and into the same number of words, in most cases, almost impossible. The difficulty is increased with HEINE'S poems, owing to the careful reduction in them of every phrase to the fewest possible words.

TRANSLATOR.

On Tuesday, in their castle,
  My ladies gave a ball;
And thither, with coaches and horses,
  Went my neighbors, their wives and all.

But I had no invitation:—
  Which bothered you, by-the-by!—
And the gossiping aunts and cousins
  Observed it, and laughed on the sly.

18.

Am fernen Horizonte.

FAR on the dim horizon,
  As in a land of dreams,
Rises a white-towered city,
  Fading 'mid sunset gleams.

The evening breeze is wreathing
  The water where I float;
And in solemn measure the sailor
  Keeps time as he rows my boat.

Again the sun is rising
  Bright-gleaming o'er the coast,
And shows the place more clearly
  Where the one I loved was lost.

19.

Sei mir gegrüßt, du Große.

ONCE more in solemn ditty
  I greet thee, as I melt

In tears, O wondrous city
 Where once my true love dwelt.

Say on, ye gates and tower,
 Does she I loved remain?
I gave her to your power:
 Give me my love again!

Blame not the trusty tower!
 No word his walls could say,
As a pair, with their trunks and baggage,
 So silently travelled away.

But the wicket-gate was faithless
 Through which she escaped so still:
Oh, a wicket is always ready
 To ope when the wicked will.*

20.

So wandl' ich wieder den alten Weg.

AGAIN through the streets well known of old
 I wander with footsteps weary;
Again before her house I come,
 And the house is empty and dreary.

---

* *Die Thore jedoch, die liessen*
 Mein Liebchen entwischen gar still;
Ein Thor ist immer willig,
 Wenn eine Thörinn will.

"A gate is ever found willing
 To let a fool "gang her ain gait."—BOWRING.

The streets are all so narrow here!
  The pavement seems to tear me!
The roofs are falling! I haste away
  As fast as my feet will bear me.

21.

Ich trat in jene Hallen.

I ENTERED her home, recalling
  The faith she had pledged while weeping:
Where I saw her tear-drops falling,
  I now found serpents creeping.

22.

Still ist die Nacht, es ruhen die Gassen.

CALM is the night, and the city is sleeping:—
  Once in this house dwelt a lady fair;
Long, long ago she left it, weeping,
  But still the old house is standing there.

Yonder a man at the heavens is staring,
  Wringing his hands as in sorrowful case;
He turns to the moonlight, his countenance baring:—
  O heaven! he shows me my own sad face!

Shadowy form, with my own agreeing,
  Why mockest thou thus, in the moonlight cold,
The sorrows which here once vexed my being
  Many a night in the days of old?

23.

Wie kannst du ruhig schlafen.

HOW canst thou sleep so calmly,
While I alive remain?
Old griefs may yet be wakened,
And then I'll break my chain.

Remember the wild old ballad,
How a dead, forgotten slave
Came to his silent lady
And bore her to the grave.

Believe me, my wondrous lovely
And wondrously gentle maid,
I live, and still am stronger
Than any who are dead.

24.

Die Jungfrau schläft in der Kammer.

THE maiden sleeps in her chamber,
The moonlight steals quivering in;
Without there's a ringing and singing,
As of waltzing about to begin.

"I will see who it is 'neath my window,
That gives me this strange serenade!"
She saw a pale skeleton figure,
Who fiddled, and sang as he played:

"A waltz you once did promise,
And have broken your word, my fair.

To-night there's a ball in the churchyard:
  So come; I will dance with you there!"

A spell came over the maiden,
  She neither could speak nor stay;
So she followed the Form,—which, singing,
  And fiddling, went dancing away,

Fiddling, and dancing, and hopping,
  And rattling his arms and spine,
The white skull grinning and nodding
  Away in the dim moonshine.

25.

Ich stand in dunkeln Träumen.

I STOOD in shadowy dreaming,
  I gazed upon her form;
And in that face, so dearly loved,
  Strange life began to warm.

And on her soft and childlike mouth
  There played a heavenly smile;
Though in her dark and lustrous eyes
  A tear-drop shone the while.

And my own tears were flowing,
  In silent agony;
For, oh! it is not possible
  That thou art lost to me.

26.

Ich unglückſel'ger Atlas! eine Welt.

I, a most wretched Atlas, who a world
Of bitterest griefs and agonies must carry,
And bear the all-unbearable, till, breaking,
The heart is lost within me.

Wild daring heart!—it was thine own mad choice:
Thou wouldst be happy, infinitely happy,
Or wretched beyond measure. Daring heart,
Now thou art truly wretched!

27.

Die Jahre kommen und gehen.

AGES may come and vanish,
Races may pass away,
But the love which I have cherished,
Within, can ne'er decay.

Once more I fain would see thee,
And kneel where'er thou art,
And, dying, whisper,—"*Madam,*
Be pleased to accept my heart!"

28.

Mir träumte: ſchaurig ſchaute der Mond.

IT seemed that the pale moon sadly shone,
And the stars were sadly gleaming:
I was borne away to my own love's town,
A hundred leagues,—while dreaming.

I came to the house where she had slept;
  I kissed the stair while weeping,—
Where often her little foot had stept,
  Which had known her garment's sweeping.

Long was the night, cold was the night;
  I sat there, chilled, despairing;
From the window looked a phantom white,
  At the chilly moonlight staring.

29.

Was will diese einsame Thräne?

WHAT means this lonely tear-drop
  Which dims mine eye to-day?
It is the last now left me,
  Where once so many lay.

It had full many a sister
  Which rolled in glittering light;
But now, with my smiles and sorrow,
  They're lost in wind and night.

And, like the mists, have faded
  The light blue sparkling stars
Which flashed their joys or sorrows
  Down through life's prison-bars.

O love,—wild love,—where art thou?
  Fled like an idle breath:
My silent, lonely tear-drop,
  Go fade in misty death!

30.

Der bleiche, herbstliche Halbmond.

THE pale half-moon is floating
  Like a boat mid cloudy waves:
Lone lies the pastor's cottage
  Amid the silent graves.

The mother reads in the Bible,
  The son seems weary and weak,
The eldest daughter is drowsy,
  While the youngest begins to speak:

"Ah me! how every minute
  Rolls by so drearily!
Only when some one is buried
  Have we any thing here to see!"

The mother murmured, while reading,
  "Thou'rt wrong: they've brought but four
Since thy poor father was buried
  Out there by the churchyard door."

The eldest daughter says, gaping,
  "No more will I hunger by you:
I'll go to the Baron to-morrow:
  He's wealthy, and fond of me too."

The son bursts out into laughter:
  "Three hunters carouse in the Sun:
They all can make gold, and gladly
  Will show me how it is done."

The mother holds the Bible
  To his pale face in grief:
"And wilt thou, wicked fellow,
  Become a highway thief?"

A rapping is heard on the window,
  There trembles a warning hand;
Without, in his black church-garments,
  They see their dead father stand.

31.

Das ist ein schlechtes Wetter.

TO-NIGHT we have dreadful weather,
  It rains and snows and storms;
I sit at my window, gazing
  Out on benighted forms.

There glimmers a lonely candle,
  Which wearily wanders on:
An old dame with a lantern
  Comes hobbling slowly anon.

—It seems that for eggs and butter,
  And sugar, she forth has come,
To make a cake for her daughter,
  Her grown-up darling at home,

Who, at the bright lamp blinking,
  In an arm-chair lazily lies;
And golden locks are waving
  Above her beautiful eyes.

32.

Man glaubt, daß ich mich gräme.

THEY say that my heart is breaking
With love and sorrow too;
And at last I shall believe it,
As other people do.

Sweet girl, with eyes dark beaming,
I have ever told thee this,
That my heart with love is breaking,
That thou wert all my bliss.

But only in my chamber
Dared I thus boldly speak:
Alas!—when thou wert present
My words were sad and weak.

For there were evil angels
Who quickly hushed my tongue;
And, oh! such evil angels
Kill many a heart when young.

33.

Deine weichen Lilienfinger.

OH, thy lovely lily-fingers!
If I once again could kiss them,
Press them once upon my heart,
And then die in silent weeping!

For thy clear deep eyes like violets
Sweep before me day and night;
And I vex my soul in guessing
At the soft, sweet, blue enigmas.

34.

Hat sie sich denn nie geäußert?

"HAS she really never noticed
That you long with love were burning?
Saw you never in her glances
Any sign of love returning?

"Could you never with your glances
Wake *that* glance which thrills and flatters,—
You, who surely are no donkey,
Friend of mine, in these small matters?"

35.

Sie liebten sich beide, doch keiner.

THEY tenderly loved, and yet neither
Would venture the other to move;
They met as if hate were between them,
And yet were half dying with love.

They parted, and then saw each other,
At times, in their visions alone;
They had long left this sad life together,
Yet scarcely to either 'twas known.

36.

Und als ich Euch meine Schmerzen geklagt.

WHEN first my afflictions you heard me rehearse,
You gaped and you stared:—God be praised 'twas no worse!
But when I repeated them smoothly in rhyme,
You thought it was "wonderful!" "glorious!" "sublime!"

37.

Ich rief den Teufel und er kam.

I CALLED the Devil, and he came:
In blank amaze his form I scanned.
He is not ugly, is not lame,
But a refined, accomplished man,—
One in the very prime of life,
At home in every cabinet strife,
Who, as diplomatist, can tell
Church and State news extremely well.
He is somewhat pale,—and no wonder, either,
Since he studies Sanscrit and Hegel together.
His favorite poet is still *Fouqué.*
Of criticism he makes no mention,
Since all such matters unworthy attention
He leaves to his grandmother, HECATÉ.
He praised my legal efforts, and said
That he also when younger some law had read,
Remarking that friendship like mine would be
An acquisition, and bowed to me,—

Then asked if we had not met before,
  At the Spanish minister's *soirée?*
And, as I scanned his face once more,
  I found I had known him for many a day!

38.

Mensch, verspotte nicht den Teufel.

MORTAL! sneer not at the Devil:
    Soon thy little life is o'er;
And eternal grim damnation
  Is no idle tale of yore.

Mortal! pay the debts thou owest:
  Long 'twill be ere life is o'er;
Many a time thou yet must borrow,
  As thou oft hast done before.

39.

Die heil'gen drei Könige aus Morgenland.

"WHICH is the way to Bethlehem?
    Is there no one to show it?"
So asked the Three Kings from the Eastern land:
  "Dear children, do you know it?"

Neither old nor young could tell them the road.
  The kings went on. Before them
There went a beautiful golden star,
  Which gleamed in its glory o'er them.

The star stood still over Joseph's house:
  They entered, their offerings bringing.
The oxen lowed, the Infant cried,
  While the three wise kings were singing.

40.

Mein Kind, wir waren Kinder,
Zwei Kinder klein und froh.

MY child, we once were children,
  Two children gay and small;
We crept into the hen-house
  And hid ourselves, heads and all.

We clucked just like the poultry;
  And when folks came by, you know,—
Kickery-kee!—they started,
  And thought 'twas a real crow.

The chests which lay in our court-yard
  We papered so smooth and nice;
We thought they were splendid houses,
  And lived in them, snug as mice.

When the old cat of our neighbor
  Dropped in for a social call,
We made her bows and courtesies,
  And compliments, and all.

We asked of her health, and kindly
  Inquired how all had sped:—
Since then to many a tabby
  The selfsame things we've said.

And oft, like good old people,
We talked with sober tongue,
Declaring that all was better
In the days when we were young;—

How piety, faith, and true love
Had vanished quite away,
And how dear we found the coffee,
How scarce the money, to-day!

So all goes rolling onward,
The merry days of youth,—
Money, the world and its seasons,
And honesty, love, and truth.

41.

Das Herz ist mir bedrückt, und sehnlich.

MY heart is sad, and with misgiving
I ponder o'er the ancient day
When this poor world was fit to live in
And calmly sped the time away.

Now all seems changed which once was cherished:
The world is filled with care and dread;
As if the Lord in heaven had perished,
And down below the Devil were dead.

But care of all hath so bereft us,
So little pleasure Life can give,
That, were not some faint *Love* still left us,
No more I'd wish on Earth to live.

42.

Wie der Mond sich leuchtend dränget.

AS the summer moon shines rising
  Through the dark and cloud-like trees,
So my soul through shadowy memories
  Still a gleaming picture sees.

All upon the deck were seated,
  Proudly sailing on the Rhine;
And the shores in summer verdure
  Gleamed in sunset's crimson shine.

And I rested, gently musing,
  At a lovely lady's feet;
And her dear pale face was gleaming
  In the sun-rays soft and fleet.

Lutes were ringing, boys were singing,
  Wondrous rapture o'er me stole;
Bluer, bluer grew the heavens,
  Fuller, higher, swelled my soul.

Like a legend, wood and river,
  Hill and tower, before me fly;
And I see the whole, reflected,
  In the lovely lady's eye.

43.

Im Traum sah ich die Geliebte.

IN dreams I saw the loved one,
  A sorrowing, wearied form,

Her beauty blanched and withered
  By many a dreary storm.

A babe on her arm she carried,
  Another by hand she led;
And poverty and trouble
  In glance and in garb I read.

She trembled through the market,
  And face to face we met;
And I calmly said, while sadly
  Her eyes on mine were set,

"Come to my house, poor sufferer,
  For you are pale and thin;
And for you by my labor
  Both meat and drink I'll win.

"And to your little children
  I'll be a father mild;
But, most of all, *your* parent,
  My poor unhappy child.

"Nor will I ever whisper
  That once I held you dear;
And if you die before me,
  I'll weep upon your bier."

44.

Theurer Freund, was soll es nützen.

FRIEND of mine, why are you ever
  Through the same old measures moving?

Will you, brooding, sit forever
  On the same old eggs of loving?

'Tis an endless incubation;
  From their eggs the chicks scarce risen,
When the chirping generation
  In a book you coop and prison.

45.

Werdet nur nicht ungedul dig.

BUT, I pray, be not impatient
  At the same old chords still ringing,
If you find the same old sorrows
  In the newest songs I'm singing.

Wait; for ye shall *yet* hear fading
  All this echo of my sorrow,
When a fresher spring of poems
  Bubbles from my heart to-morrow.

46.

Nun ist es Zeit, daß ich mit Verstand.

IT is time that my mind from this folly I free,—
  Yes, time I were guided by reason:
You've been playing the part of an actor with me,
  I fear, for too lengthened a season.

In the warmest style of the highest romance,
  Our scenery all was new-fangled:

I thought but of lady, of helm, and of lance,
  And my armor was splendidly spangled.

But I sigh now to think that such parts I could fill,
  With this frippery lying before me;
And a feeling as though I played comedy still
  Comes wretchedly wandering o'er me.

Ah, Heaven! I spoke what in secret I felt;
  Unconscious I did it, and jesting;
As the Dying Athlete before you I knelt,
  While Death in my own heart was resting.

47.

Den König Wiswamitra.

THE great king *Wiswa-mitra*
  Is lost in trouble now;
For he through strife and penance
  Would win *Waschischta's* cow.

O great king *Wiswa-mitra!*
  Oh, what an ass art thou
To bear such strife and penance
  All for a single cow!

48.

Herz, mein Herz, sei nicht beklommen.

HEART, my heart, oh, be not shaken,
  And still calmly bear thy pain!
  For the spring will bring again
What a dreary winter's taken.

And how much is still remaining,
And how bright the world still beams!
And, my heart, what pleasant seems
Thou mayst love with none complaining.

49.

Du bist wie eine Blume.

THOU'RT like a lovely floweret,
So void of guile or art.
I gaze upon thy beauty,
And grief steals o'er my heart.

I fain would lay, devoutly,
My hands upon thy brow,
And pray that God will keep thee
As good and fair as now.

50.

Kind! es wäre dein Verderben.

CHILD! it were your utter ruin,
And I strive, right earnestly,
That your gentle heart may never
Glow with aught like love for me.

But the thought that 'twere so easy
Still amid my dreams will move me,
And I still am ever thinking
That 'twere sweet to make you love me.

51.

Wenn ich auf dem Lager liege.

WHEN on my bed I'm lying,
At night, on pillows warm,
There ever floats before me
A sweet and gentle form.

But soon as silent slumber
Has closed my weary eyes,
Before me, in a vision,
I see the image rise.

Yet with the dream of morning
It will not pass away,
For I bear it in my bosom
Around, the live-long day.

52.

Mädchen mit dem rothen Mündchen.

MAIDEN with thy mouth of roses,
And with eyes serene and bright!
Thou, my little darling maiden,
Dearest to my heart and sight!

Long the winter nights are growing :—
Would I might forget their gloom,
By thee sitting, with thee chatting,
In thy little friendly room!

Often to my lips, in rapture,
I would press thy snowy hand,
Often with my eyes bedewing
Silently that darling hand.

53.

Mag da draußen Schnee sich thürmen.

THOUGH, without, the snow-drifts tower,
Though hail falls, and tempests shower,
On the window-pane loud rattling,
Little will I heed their battling;
For her form will ever bring
To my heart the joys of spring.

54.

Andre beten zur Madonne.

MANY pray to the Madonna,
Others run to Paul or Peter:
I will only pray to you, love,
Fairest sun of starry women!

Grant me kisses!—you have won me!
Oh, be merciful and gracious,
Fairest sun among the maidens,
'Neath the sun, of girls the fairest!

55.

Verrieth mein blasses Angesicht.

AND do not my pale cheeks betray
The pains at heart distressing?

And would you hear so proud a mouth
  The beggar's prayer confessing?

Ah me! this mouth is far too proud;
  It knows but jests and kisses,
And may have spoken mocking words
  To hide the heart's distresses.

56.

Theurer Freund, du bist verliebt.

DEAREST friend, you are in love;
  Tighter draws the chain, and tighter;
In your head 'tis getting dark,
  While your heart is growing lighter.

Dearest friend, you are in love;
  Yet from confidence you're turning,
When I see your glowing heart
  Through your very waistcoat burning!

57.

Ich wollte bei dir weilen.

I FAIN would linger near thee,
  But, when I sought to woo,
There was no time to hear me:
  There was "too much to do."

I told you, shortly after,
  That all your own I'd be;

And, with a peal of laughter,
You made a courtesy.

At last you did confuse me
More utterly than this;
For you did even refuse me
A trifling parting kiss!

Fear not that I shall languish,
Or shoot myself:—oh, no!
I've gone through all this anguish
Quite often, long ago.

58.

Saphire sind die Augen dein.

BRIGHT sapphires are your beaming eyes,
Dear eyes, so softly greeting:
Ah me! thrice happy is the man
Whom they with love are meeting.

Your heart's a diamond, bright and clear,
Whence rays of light are flowing:
Ah me! thrice happy is the man
For whom with love they're glowing.

Your lips are rubies, melting red;
No brighter need we seek:
Ah me! thrice happy is the man
To whom with love they speak.

Oh, if I knew that happy man,
  Oh, could I find the lover,
Then all alone in the gay greenwood:
  His joys would soon be over.

59.

Habe mich mit Liebesreden
Fest gelogen an dein Herz.

WITH love-vows I long have bound me,
  Firmly tied me, to thy heart;
Now, with my own meshes round me,
  Jesting turns to pain and smart.

But if thou—with right before thee—
  Now shouldst turn away thy head,
Then the devil would soon come o'er me,
  And, by Jove, I'd shoot me dead!

60.

Zu fragmentarisch ist Welt und Leben.

THIS world and this life are so scattered, they try me;
  And so to a German professor I'll hie me.
He can well put all the fragments together
  Into a system, convenient and terse;
While with his night-cap and dressing-robe tatters
  He'll stop up the chinks of the wide Universe.

61.

Sie haben heut Abend Gesellschaft.

TO-NIGHT they give a party.
  The house gleams bright above;
And across the lighted window
  I see your shadow move.

You see me not in the darkness;
  I stand alone, apart;
Still less can you cast your glances
  Into my gloomy heart.

This gloomy heart still loves you;
  It loves,—though long forgot.
Breaking, convulsed, and bleeding,
  Alas! you see it not!

62.

Ich wollt' meine Schmerzen ergössen
Sich all' in ein einziges Wort.

I WOULD I could blend my sorrows
  All into a single word:
It should fly on the wilful breezes
  As wildly as a bird.

They should carry to thee, my loved one,
  That saddest, strangest word:
At every hour it would meet thee,
  In every place be heard.

And as soon as those eyes in slumber
  Had dimmed their starry gleam,
That word of my sorrow should follow
  Down to thy deepest dream.

63.

Du hast Diamanten und Perlen,
Hast Alles was Menschen begehr'.

THOU hast diamonds, and dresses, and jewels,
  And all that a mortal could crave;
Thou hast eyes that are fairer than any,
  My dearest!—what more wouldst thou have?

To those eyes which are brighter than jewels
  I have written—both lively and grave—
An army of poems immortal,
  My dearest!—what more wouldst thou have?

Ah! those eyes which are brighter than diamonds
  Have brought me wellnigh to the grave:
I am tortured, tormented, and ruined,
  My dearest!—what more wouldst thou have?

64.

Wer zum ersten Male liebt.

HE who for the first time loves,
  Though unloved, is still a god;
But the man who loves a second,
And in vain, must be a fool.

Such a fool am I, now loving
Once again, without return:
Sun and moon and stars are smiling,
And I smile with them,—and perish.

65.

Zu der Lauheit und der Flauheit
Deiner Seele paßte nicht.

NO! the tameness and the sameness
Of your soul would not agree
With my own soul's ruder braveness,
Which o'er rocks went leaping free.

Your love-paths were graded turnpikes:
Now with husband, every day,
Arm-in-arm I see you walking
Bravely,—in the family way!

66.

Gaben mir Rath und gute Lehren.

THEY gave me advice which I scarcely heeded,
Piled on me praises I never needed,
Said that I only should "wait a while,"
Offered their patronage, too, with a smile.

But, with all their honor and approbation,
I should long ago have died of starvation,
Had there not come an excellent man,
Who bravely to help me along began.

Good fellow!—he got me the food I ate;
His kindness and care I shall never forget:
Yet I cannot embrace him, though *other* folks *can*,
For I myself am this excellent man!

67.

Diesen liebenswürd'gen Jüngling.

I CAN never speak too highly
  Of this amiable young fellow;
Oft he treated me to oysters,
  Good old hock, and cordials mellow.

Neatly fit his coat and trousers;
  His cravats are worth admiring;
And he sees me every morning,
  Of my state of health inquiring,

Of my great renown still speaking,
  Of my wit and condescension,
And to aid me or to serve me
  Does his best without pretension.

Every evening to the ladies,
  In the tones of one inspired,
He declaims my "heavenly poems,
  Which the world has so admired."

Oh, but is it not refreshing
  Still to find such persons flying,—
And in times like these, when truly
  All the better sort seem dying?

68.

Mir träumt': ich bin der liebe Gott.

I DREAMED that I was Lord of all,
High up in heaven sitting,
With cherubim who praised my song
Around in glory flitting.

And cakes I ate, and sugar-plums,
Worth many a shining dollar;
And claret-punch I also drank,
With never a bill to follow.

And yet ennui vexed me sore:
I longed for earthly revel;
And, were I not the Lord himself,
I'd gladly been the Devil.

"Come, trot, tall Angel Gabriel,
To thee broad wings are given;
Go find my dearest friend *Eugene*,
And bring him up to heaven!

"Ask not for him in lecture-rooms,
But where Tokay inspires;
Seek him not in the Hedwig's church,
Seek him at Ma'mselle Meyer's!"

Abroad he spreads his mighty wings,
To earth his course descends;
He catches up the astonished youth
Right from among his friends.

"Yes, youth, I now am Lord of all,
The earth is my possession;
I always told you I was bound
To rise in my profession.

"And miracles I too can work,
To set you wild with pleasure:
And now I'll make the town Ix-Ix*
Rejoice beyond all measure.

"For every stone which paves the street
Shall now be split in two,
And in the midst shall sparkle bright
An oyster fresh as dew.

"A gentle shower of lemon-juice
Shall give the oysters savor;
The gutters of the streets must run
With hock of extra flavor."

How the Ix-Ixers go to work!
What cries of joy they utter!
The council and the aldermen
Are swilling up the gutter.

And how the poets all rejoice,
To see things done so neatly!
The ensigns, and lieutenants too,
Have cleaned the streets completely.

---

* Or X, x. In one edition HEINE calls this town *Berlin*. TRANSLATOR.

The wisest are the officers ;
  For, speculation scorning,
They sagely say, "Such miracles
  Don't happen every morning."

69.

Von schönen Lippen fortgedrängt, getrieben.

FROM sweetest lips have I been forced, and driven
  From fairest arms and beauty captivating:
Long had I gladly rested in this heaven,
  But—with his horses stood the post-boy, waiting!

And such is life, my child;—an endless plaining,
  A long adieu, a lasting parting hour.
Could not your heart charm mine into remaining?
  Could not your glances keep me by their power?

70.

*Wir fuhren allein im dunkeln
Postwagen die ganze Nacht.*

WE rode in the dark post-carriage,
  We travelled all night alone;
We slept and we jested together,
  We laughed until morning shone.

But as daylight came dawning o'er us,
  My dear, how we started to find

Between us a traveller, named Cupid,
Who had ventured on "going it blind"!*

71.

Das weiß Gott, wo sich die tolle
Dirne einquartiret hat.

LORD knows where the wild young hussy
Whom I seek has settled down.
Swearing at the rain and weather,
I have scoured through all the town.

I have run from inn to tavern,—
Ne'er a bit of news I gain,—
And of every saucy waiter
I've inquired,—and all in vain.

---

* *Doch als es Morgens tagte,*
Mein Kind, wie staunten wir!
Denn zwischen uns sass Amor,
Der blinde Passagier.

I have heard "a blind passenger" described as the one who sits at the end of the *Eilwagen* (or Diligence), where there is no window. But, in popular parlance, "the blind passenger" is one who—to translate a bit of German slang by its American equivalent—may be termed a "self-elected dead-head," an individual who slips in and out of an entertainment, coach, steamboat, or the like, without paying for his admission, or one not included in the regular list.

Literally this verse reads, "But when day dawned, my child, how we were astonished! for between us sat *Amor*, the blind passenger."—Translator.

There she is! at yonder window,—
Smiling, beckoning to me. Well,
How was I to know you quartered,
Miss, in such a grand hotel?

72.

Und bist du erst mein ehlich Weib.

WHEN you become my married wife,
You'll be my envied treasure;
You'll have the very merriest life,
With nothing but joy and pleasure.

And if the very devil you raise,
I'll bear it in silent sorrow;
But if you fail my verse to praise,
I'll be divorced o' the morrow.

73.

Wie dunkle Träume stehen
Die Häuser in langer Reih'.

LIKE dusky dreams, the houses
Stand in a lengthened row;
And, wrapped in my Spanish mantle,
Through the shadow I silently go.

The tower of the old cathedral
Announces that midnight has come;

And now, with her charms and her kisses,
  My dearest is waiting at home.

The moon is my boon companion:
  She cheerily lights my way,
Till I come to the house of my true love;
  And then to the moon I say,

"Many thanks for your light, old comrade;
  Receive my parting bow;
For the rest of the night I'll excuse you:
  Go shine upon other folks now.

"And if you should light on a lover
  Who drearily sorrows alone,
Console him as you have consoled me
  In the wearisome times long gone."

74.

In den Küssen, welche Lüge.

WHAT lies are hid in kisses,
  What delight in mere parade!
To betray may have its blisses,
  But more blest is the betrayed.

Say what thou wilt, my fairest,
  Still I know what thou'lt receive:
I'll believe just what thou swearest,
  And will swear what thou'lt believe.

75.

Auf deinem schneeweißen Busen.

UPON your snowy bosom
  I laid my weary head,
And secretly I listened
  To what the heart-throbs said.

The blue hussars come riding,
  With trumpets, to the gate;
And to-morrow she who loves me
  Will seek another mate.

But, though you leave to-morrow,
  To-day you still must rest;
And in those lovely arms, love,
  Will I be doubly blest.

76.

Es blasen die blauen Husaren.

BLUE hussars with their trumpets loud sounding
  Through the town-gate are riding away:
So again to you, darling, I'm bringing
  Fresh roses,—a lovely bouquet.

Oh, that was the craziest business!
  Much trouble in every part;
And many a dashing blade was "drawn"
  And "quartered" in your heart.

77.

Habe auch in jungen Jahren.

I TOO, in life's early season,
Had my pains beyond all reason,
From love's burning mood;
But now I find that wood is dear,
The fire burns lower every year,
Ma foi!—and that is good.

Think of that, my dear young beauty;
Dry your tears, since joy is duty;
Heed no false alarms:
While your veins with young life quiver,
Let the old love fade forever,
Ma foi!—in my fond arms.

78.

Selten habt ihr mich verstanden.

SELDOM did we know each other,
Seldom were you understood;
But our souls soon came together
When we met in filth and mud.

79.

Doch die Kastraten klagten.

HOW the eunuchs were complaining
At the roughness of my song!
Complaining and explaining
That my voice was much too strong.

Then, delicately thrilling,
They all began to sing:
Like crystal was their trilling,
So pure it seemed to ring.

They sang of *passion* sweeping
In hot floods from the heart:
The ladies all were weeping,
In a rapturous sense of Art!

80.

Ich hab' Euch im besten Juli verlassen.

'TWAS just in the midst of July that I left you,
And now in mid-winter I meet you once more;
Then, as we parted, with heat ye were glowing,
Now ye are cool, and the fever is o'er.

Once more I leave. Should I come again hither,
Then you will be neither burning nor cold:
Over your graves—well-a-day!—I'll be treading,
And find that my own heart is weary and old!

81.

Neben mir wohnt Don Henriquez.

NEAR to me lives Don Henriquez,
As "the handsome" celebrated:
Neighboring are our apartments,
By a thin wall separated.

Salamanca's loveliest ladies,
When he walks, are gloating o'er him,—

Rattling spurs and curled mustachios,
  And his hounds, of course, before him.

But in silent summer evenings
  Calm at home he sits, half dreaming,
Touching his guitar and humming,
  O'er his soul sweet fancies streaming.

Now he sweeps the strings more strongly,
  Loudly thrill his wild romances:—
Worse to me than drunken headaches
  Are his snarling quavering fancies!

82.

Auf den Wällen Salamanka's.

ROUND the walls of Salamanca
  Soft the summer breeze is blowing:
There I wander with my Donna,
  When the evening red is glowing.

Round the lady's slender body
  My embracing arm still lingers;
And I feel her bosom proudly
  Swelling, with my happy fingers.

Yet a murmur, as of anguish,
  Through the linden-boughs is streaming,
And the gloomy stream below us
  Murmurs, as if evil dreaming.

Ah, Señora! dark forebodings
  Of "expulsion" round are stalking:
On the walls of Salamanca
  We no more can then go walking.

83.

Bist du wirklich mir so feindlich?

NOW then, do you really hate me?
  Are you really changed so sadly?
I'll complain to everybody
  That you've treated me so badly.

O ye red lips, so ungrateful,
  Say, how could ye speak unkindly
Of the man who kissed so warmly,
  And of him who loved so blindly?

84.

Ach, die Augen sind es wieder.

STILL the same those eyes beguiling,
  Which once lent to love completeness;
Still the same those soft lips smiling,
  Which to life gave all its sweetness.

Still the same that voice, whose music
  I have listened to with yearning:
But I am the same no longer,
  Changed so strangely since returning.

By the fair white arms so firmly,
  Passionately, now surrounded,
I upon her heart am lying,
  Melancholy and confounded.

85.

Kaum sahen wir uns, und an Augen und Stimme.

SCARCE had we met, when, in tones and in glances,
  I saw that you liked me, and nothing was missed;
And had not your mother been there with her fancies,
  Right certain I am that at once we'd have kissed.

To-morrow I'll leave, while the world will be sleeping;
  Away, as of old, on my journey I'll go;
And then my blonde girl from the window 'll be peeping,
  And glances of love at the window I'll throw.

86.

Ueber die Berge steigt schon die Sonne.

THE sunlight is stealing o'er mountain and river,
  The cries of the flocks are heard over the plain;
My love and my lamb and my darling forever,
  How glad I would be could I see thee again!

Upwards I look, and with glances full loving,
  "Darling, adieu! I must wander from thee."
Vainly I wait, for no curtain is moving:
  She lies and she sleeps, and she's dreaming of me.

87.

Nacht liegt auf den fremden Wegen.

ON strange roads the night is lying,
  Weariness and pain before me!
When, like blessings softly flying,
  The sweet moon-rays quiver o'er me.

Gentle moon, by that bright gleaming
  Nightly terrors soon you banish;
And my eyes with tears are streaming,
  As my fears and sorrows vanish.

88.

Zu Halle auf dem Markt.

IN the market-place of Halle
  There stand two mighty lions:
O thou lion-pride of Halle,
  How greatly art thou tamed!

In the market-place of Halle
  There stands a mighty giant;
He hath a sword, yet never stirs,—
  He's petrified with terror.

In the market-place of Halle
  A mighty church is standing,
Where the *Burschenschaft* and the *Landsmann-*
    *schaft**
  Have plenty of room for praying.

---

* Student Associations, the *Burschenschaft* being general and political in its objects, while the *Landsmannschafter* are local.
TRANSLATOR.

89.

Dämmernd liegt der Sommerabend.

SUMMER eve with day is striving,
Softly gaining wood and meadow;
Mid blue heavens the golden moonlight
Gleams, in perfumed air reviving.

Crickets round the brooks are cheeping;
Something stirs amid the water;
And the wanderer hears a plashing,
And a breath amid the sleeping:

There alone, beside the river,
See! a fair Undine is bathing:
Arms and bosom, white and lovely,
In the shimmering moon-rays quiver.

90.

Der Tod das ist die kühle Nacht.

DEATH is a cool and pleasant night,
Life is a sultry day.
'Tis growing dark,—I'm weary;
For day has tired me with his light.

Over my bed a fair tree gleams,
And in it sits a nightingale:
She sings of naught save love:
I hear it even in dreams.

91.

Sag', wo ist dein schönes Liebchen.

SAY, where is your own fair darling,
  Whom you once were sweetly singing,
When the flames of magic power
  Strangely through your heart were springing?

Ah! those flames no more are burning,
  And my cold heart feels no flashes,
And this book's the urn containing
  Of that love the dreary ashes.

92.

THE TWILIGHT OF THE GODS.

Der Mai ist da mit seinen goldnen Lichten.

THE month of May with golden gleams is coming,
  With silken breezes and with spicy odors,
And, loving, laughing, lures with blanching blossoms,
From deep-blue violet eyes by thousands greets us,
And spreads around her green and flowery carpet,
With warp of sunshine and the morning dew,
And calls around her darling human children.
Even her first call the bashful folk obey:
The men put on their nankeen pantaloons,
And Sunday coats with glittering golden buttons,
The dames adorn themselves with innocent white,
Young men curl up with care their spring moustaches,
Young ladies let their bosoms heave in freedom,

And the town-poets put into their pockets
Paper and pencil and lorgnette, and joyous
Go to the gate the various moving crowd,
And, on the green bank comfortably lying,
They wonder at the trees industrious growing,
Play with the delicate many-colored flowers,
List to the merry birds above them singing,
And gayly whoop to tho blue heaven's arch.

To me the May came too. Three times she knocked
Upon my door, and cried, "Lo, I am May.
O poor, pale dreamer, come, and I will kiss you!"
I kept my door fast bolted, and I cried,
"In vain you tempt me forth, O evil guest!
I have seen through you, and I have seen through
The fabric of the world, and seen too much
And far too deeply, and all joys are gone,
And endless pains are flowing through my heart.
I have seen through the shells, so hard and stony,
Of human homes, and hearts which are called human,
And seen in either lies, deceit, and sorrow.
I read in thoughts of men upon their faces
Much that is evil. In the virgin's blushes
I see hot lust in secret yearnings quiver;
And on the proud head of a youth inspired
I see the motley and the mocking fool's cap;
And folly's fevered forms and sickly shadows
I see upon this earth; and so I know not
If earth's a house for lazars, or a mad-house.
And I can see through the old earth's foundations,
As though they were of crystal,—and the horrors

Which with a joyous verdure still to cover
Sweet May strives all in vain. I see the dead, too;
There they all lie, hid in their narrow coffins,
With stiff and folded hands, and eyes wide open,
While through their yellow lips the worms are creeping.
I see the son with a gay sweetheart sitting,
And all in joke, upon a father's grave:—
The nightingales sing mocking songs around them;
The softest meadow-flowers laugh with malice:
The poor dead father turns him in his grave,
And our old mother earth in sharp pain quivers.

Poor earth of ours, how well I know thy torture!
I see the hot fire in thy bosom heaving,
I see thy thousand veins in anguish bleeding,
And mark thy gaping wounds again torn open,
And wild up-streaming flame and smoke and blood.
I see thy scornful, daring, giant children,
The dark primeval brood, from black abysses
Rising, and rising still, flashing red torches,
Raising their iron ladders ever up,
And storming headlong to the towers of heaven,
Their black dwarfs hurrying on. With thunder crashing,
The golden stars shiver to shining dust,
And whirl away to nothing; bolder still,
They tear the curtain from the tent of God:
The gentle angels wail, and fly in swarms
Headlong in horror. And upon his throne
The pale God sits, and casts afar his crown,
And tears his hair while the hell-host roars on,

And the mad giants cast their blood-red torches
O'er the wide realm of heaven, and the goblins
Cut with keen scourging flames the angels' backs,
Who twist and twine in very agony,
And then are slung afar by their fair tresses.
And I do see my guardian angel there,
With his fair flowing locks and dear sweet features,
The smile of love eternal on his lips,
And heaven's bliss beaming in those blue eyes;
And, lo! a hateful, horrid, swarthy devil
Up-tears him from the earth, my poor, pale angel,
And, grinning, glares upon his noble figure,
And twines around in tenderest embraces!
A yelling scream pierces the universe:
Their pillars breaking, Earth and Heaven mingle,
And now the ancient Night is lord of all.

93.

RATCLIFF.

Der Traumgott brachte mich in eine Landschaft.

THE Dream-God brought me to a rural scene,
Where weeping willows waved a welcome to me
With all their long green arms, and where the flowers
With shrewd, sweet sister-glances still observed me,
Where the birds' songs seemed known long, long ago,
And even the distant barking of the dogs
Was something heard before in sweet old times;
And there were forms and voices kindly greeting,
Like a long-absent friend: yet all around me

Did seem so strange, so wonderfully strange!
I stood before a handsome inland dwelling,
And all my brain was calm, though in my bosom
There was a wild commotion: yet quite calm
I shook the dust out of my travelling garments,
Harsh rang the door-bell, and the door unclosèd.

And there were men and women,—many faces
Known in the olden time. A silent sorrow
Lay with a shy and secret terror on them,
And, strangely moved, they looked, almost with pity,
Upon me, until I myself was moved
As with foreboding of an unknown evil.
Old Margaret I knew at the first glance,
And looked inquiringly; and yet she spoke not.
"Where is Maria?" I asked; and still she spoke not,
But gently took my hand, at length, and led me,
Through many a long and lighted-up apartment,
Where a dead silence tempered pomp and pride,
Until I came unto a darksome chamber,
And showed me, with her face all turned away,
The form of one who on the sofa sat.
"Are you Maria?" I asked,—and inwardly
I was myself astonished at the firmness
With which I spoke. Like stone or metal
There rang a voice: "That is what people call me."
A cutting agony froze through my veins,
For that cold, hollow tone was still the voice—
Or what had been the sweet voice—of Maria!
Yes, and that woman, in faded lilac gown
Cast on so slovenly, with hanging breasts,
With staring, glassy eyes, with every muscle

Of the white face so leather-like and dead,—
Ah! and that woman once had been the fair,
The blooming, gentle, beautiful Maria!
"You have been travelling long," she cried, aloud
And with a cold, unpleasant forwardness:
"You don't seem quite so loving, my good friend;
You are in health, and those firm loins and calves
Show a good, solid state." A sweetish smile
Then flitted round her pale and yellow mouth.
In my confusion there escaped the words,
"They tell me you are married." "Yes,—it's true!"
She said, indifferently, and with a smile:
"I've got a wooden stick in leather cased
Which calls itself a husband!—Lord!—but wood
Is wood, and nothing else." And then she laughed
Harshly and contradictingly, till I
Felt a cold terror running through my soul,
And the doubt seized on me,—Are *those* the lips,
The virgin-blossom lips, of my Maria?
But then she rose in haste, and quickly caught
Her Cashmere from a chair, and cast it on
Around her neck, then hung her on my arm,
And through the open door she led the way
Through field and grove and glen, and ever on.

The crimson-glowing disk of the late sun
Was sweeping down, flashing a purple dream
Upon the trees and flowers and the fair stream
Which far away majestically flowed.
"See how the great gold eye is shimmering
In the blue water!" cried Maria, in haste.
"Be silent, you poor creature!" I replied,

Seeing unearthly shades in the dim light:
Strange cloudy forms winding in fairy wise
Were flitting dreamily above the fields,
Ever with soft white spirit arms embracing;
And tenderly the violets looked on them,
While all the lily-cups waved down together;
Voluptuous heat in all the roses glowed,
The pinks seemed flaming in their very breath,
And all the flowers were flushed with strong perfume,
And all of them in amorous rapture wept,
And all of them cried out, "O Love! Love! Love!"
The butterflies came fluttering, and the bright
Gold-beetles hummed their droning elfin lay;
The evening breezes rustled, and the oaks
Whispered, while melting sang the nightingale;
And, mid the whispering, rustling, singing sounds,
With cold, unmusical, metallic voice
The faded woman chattered by my side:
"I know your deeds by night up in the castle.
The slender shadow's a good-natured thing,
That nods assent to every thing you will,
And Blue Coat!—he's an angel; but the Red,
With a bare sword, hates you with all his heart."
And many other strangely-mingled words
She chattered without pause, and then sat down,
Wearied, beside me, on the mossy bench
Which stands so low beneath the old oak-tree.

And there we sat together, sad and still.
Each looked at each, and either sadder grew.
The oak-tree rustled as with dying sighs;
In agony the nightingale sang down.

But a red light came shining through the leaves
And, flickering, flashed across her cold white face,
Awaking a strange glow in the glassy eyes,
And with the old sweet voice again she spoke:
"How did you know my fearful misery?
I read it lately in your wild, sad songs."

An icy coldness crept through all my breast;
At my own madness I was terrified,
Which made of me a seer. Darkness rushed in;
And, in my horror, I awoke from sleep.

94.

DONNA CLARA.

In dem abendlichen Garten.

IN the pleasant twilight garden
The Alcalde's daughter's straying:
Trump and drum from distant towers
Send their music to the maiden.

"I am weary of the dances,
Of the flattery I'm weary,
And of merry knights comparing
Me to the bright sun,—so courtly!

"Yes, of all things I am weary,
Since by moonlight gliding softly
I first saw the knight whose lute-play
Nightly to the window brought me.

"As he stood so tall and stately,
And his gleaming glances darted

From his pale and noble features,
He was like Saint George the Warder."

So reflected Donna Clara,
And, while musing, bowed her forehead.
Looking up, she saw the handsome
Unknown knight, who stood before her,

Whispering love with love's caresses,
Straying where the moon shines sweetest,
Where the breeze blows sweet assurance,
Fairy-like the roses greet them.

Fairy-like the roses greet them,
Like love's messengers red-glowing.
"But I beg you, darling, tell me
Why your cheeks are flushed and rosy."

"A mosquito stung me, darling;
And they are in summer weather
Quite as hateful things as though they
All were long-nosed Jewish wretches."

"Never mind the stings or Jews, love,"
Said the knight, caressing fondly:
"See the showers of snowy blossoms
From the almond-branches falling!"

"Showers of sweet and snowy blossoms
Pour their perfume sweetly o'er me"—
"But your heart,—is *that*, my darling,
All and all to me devoted?"

"Yes, I dearly love thee, darling;
And I swear it by the Saviour
Whom the God-accursèd Hebrews
Murdered treacherously, basely."

"Never mind the Hebrews, dearest,"
Softly wooing, said the lover:
"In the distance, dream-like waving,
Snow-white lilies gleam in glory,—

"Lilies in a light soft flowing,
Yearning to the stars above them;
But have you ne'er been false, my dearest,
To the oath you swore to love me?"

"Falsehood is not in me, darling:
In my breast no drop is running
Of the race of the Moresco,
Or of Jews so vile and dirty."

"Never mind Jews or Morescos,"
Said the knight, caressing softly.
To a sheltered grove of myrtle
He has led the Alcalde's daughter.

With the soft fine snare of passion
Daintily is Clara covered;
Short his words, but long his kisses,
And their hearts are overflowing.

Like a luscious melting bride-song
Sings dame Nightingale, the dearest;
In a merry marriage torch-dance
Glow-worms on the ground are leaping.

In the bower all is silent,
All is silent round the lovers,
Save the whispering of the myrtles,
And the flowers their breath recovering!

But the sound of drums and trumpets
From the castle-towers comes pealing,
And, awaking, Donna Clara
From his warm embraces frees her.

"Hear! they call me now, my darling!
Yet, before we part this evening,
Let me know what the dear name is
Which so long you've kept a secret."

And the lover, gayly smiling,
Kissed his lovely lady's fingers,
Kissed her lips, too, and her forehead,
And at length the words he whispers,

"I, Señora, I, your lover,
Am the son of the much-honored,
Great, and Scripture-learnèd Rabbi,
Israel of Saragoza."

95.

ALMANZOR.

In dem Dome zu Corduva.

I.

IN Cordova's grand cathedral
Stand the pillars thirteen hundred;
Thirteen hundred giant pillars
Bear the cupola, that wonder.

And on walls and dome and pillars,
From the top to bottom winding,
Flow the Arabic Koran proverbs,
Quaintly and like flowers twining.

Moorish monarchs once erected
This fair pile to Allah's glory;
But in the wild dark whirl of ages
Many a change has stolen o'er it.

On the minaret, where the Mollah
Called to prayer amid the turrets,
Now the Christian bells are ringing
With a melancholy drumming.

On the steps where once the Faithful
Sung the praises of the Prophet,
Now the mass's worn-out wonder
To the world the bald priests offer.

What a turning, what a twisting,
By the puppets in odd draping!
What a bleating, steaming, ringing,
Round the foolish, flashing tapers!

In Cordova's grand cathedral
Stands Almanzor ben Abdullah,
Silently the pillars eyeing,
And these words in silence murmuring:

"O ye strong and giant pillars,
Once adorned in Allah's glory,
Now ye serve, and deck while serving,
The detested faith now o'er us!

"But if to the times ye're suited,
And ye calmly bear the burden,
Surely it becomes the weaker
Of such lore to be a learner."

So Almanzor ben Abdullah
Smiled and bowed with cheerful motion
O'er the decorated font-stone
In the minster of Cordova.

II.

Hastig schritt er aus dem Dome.

HASTILY from the cathedral,
Headlong on his wild horse riding,
Went the knight, his ringlets waving,
And with them his feathers flying,

On the way to Alcolea,
All along the Guadalquivir,
By the perfumed golden orange
And the almond's snow-white glitter.

Onward flies the joyous rider,
Whistling, singing, gayly laughing;
And the birds with merry music,
And the waterfall, sing after.

In the castle Alcolea
Dwells fair Clara de Alvarez.
She is free now, since her father
Wages battle in Navarra.

In the distance drums and trumpets
Sound a welcome to Almanzor,
And he sees the castle-tapers
Gleaming through the forest-shadows.

In the castle Alcolea
Twelve fair dames are gayly dancing:
Twelve gay knights are dancing with them,
Best of all Almanzor dances.

As if whirled by gay caprices,
Round the hall he gayly flutters,
And by him to every lady
Sweetest flattery is uttered.

Isabella's pretty fingers
Then are kissed, and then he leaves her;
Next he stands before Elvira,
In her dark eyes archly peeping.

Laughingly he asks Lenora
If to-day he strikes her fancy;
And he shows the golden crosses
Richly broidered in his mantle.

And he vows to every lady,
"In my heart you live, believe me;"
And "as true as I'm a Christian!"
Thirty times he swore that evening.

III.

In dem Schloß zu Alcolea.

IN the castle Alcolea
Mirth and music cease their ringing;
Lords and ladies are departed,
And the tapers are extinguished.

Donna Clara and Almanzor,
Only they alone still linger:
On them shines a single taper,
With its light wellnigh extinguished.

On her chair the dame is seated,
On her footstool he is dozing;
Till his head, with slumber weary,
On the knees he loves reposes.

Now she pours attar of roses
Cautiously, from golden vial,
On the brown locks of Almanzor,
And she hears him deeply sighing.

Ever cautiously the lady
Presses kisses sweet and loving
On the brown locks of Almanzor;
But his brow is clouded over.

Ever cautiously the lady
Weeps in floods, with anguish yearning,
On the brown locks of Almanzor;
And his lip with scorn is curling.

And he dreams again he's standing
In the minster at Cordova,
Bending with his brown locks dripping,
Gloomy voices murmuring o'er him.

And he hears the giant pillars
Their impatient anger murmur:
Longer they will not endure it,
And they tremble, and they totter,

And they wildly crash together.
Deadly pale are priest and people.
Down the cupola comes thundering,
And the Christian gods are grieving.

96.

THE PILGRIMAGE TO KEVLAAR.

I.

Am Fenster stand die Mutter.

THE mother stood at the window,
In sick-bed lay her son:
"Will you not rise up, William,
Ere the pilgrim-train be gone?"

"I am so ill, O mother,—
I cannot hear or see:
I think of my dead Margaret,
And my heart is a pain to me."

"Rise! we will go to Kevlaar,
Take prayer-book and rosary:

The Mother of God will heal again
  That poor sick heart in thee."

The sacred banners are rustling,
  The solemn psalm peals high:
It was at Cologne in the Rhine-land
  That this procession went by.

The mother followed the many;
  With her sad son went she,
Both singing in the chorus,
  "Blessed be thou, Marie!"

II.

Die Mutter Gottes zu Kevlaar.

THE Virgin Mary at Kevlaar
  Puts on her best array;
For she must be right busy
  With the sick who come to-day.

And votive gifts are offered
  By many sickly bands,
Limbs all from white wax modelled,
  And waxen feet and hands.

And he who a wax hand offers,
  His hand will be free from pain;
And he who a wax foot offers,
  His foot will be well again.

To Kevlaar went many on crutches
  Who now on the tight-rope bound,
And many now play the viol
  Who had never a finger sound.

The mother took a taper,
  And made from the wax a heart:
"Take that to the Virgin Mary,
  And she will heal thy smart."

The son with the heart went sighing
  To the holy image there:
Tears from his eyes came bursting,
  And there burst from his heart the prayer:

"Thou the most highly blessed!
  God's purest handmaid thou!
And queen, too, of the heaven!
  Hear all my sorrow now!—

"I lived, along with mother,
  At Cologne, and in the town
Where are many hundred churches
  And chapels of renown.

"And near to us lived Margaret,
  Who is dead and gone away:—
Mary, I bring thee a wax heart:
  Oh, heal my heart, I pray!"

III.

Der kranke Sohn und die Mutter.

THE sickly son and his mother
  In their little chamber slept:
There came the Holy Mother,
  And softly in she stept.

Above the sick boy she bent her,
  While her hand all softly lay
Upon his breast. Sweet smiling,
  She vanished far away.

The mother saw all in dreaming,
  And more in her vision still,
Then wakened from her slumber :
  The dogs were barking shrill.

There lay at length before her
  Her son,—and he was dead!
On his pale cheeks was playing
  The gleaming morning red.

Her hands the mother folded,
  She felt she knew not how:
Softly she sang, and piously,
  "O Mary, blest art thou!"

"Nothing is permanent but change, nothing constant but death. Every pulsation of the heart inflicts a wound; and life would be an endless bleeding, were it not for Poetry. She secures to us what Nature would deny,—a golden age without rust, a spring which never fades, cloudless prosperity and eternal youth."

BÖRNE.

PROLOGUE.

Schwarze Röcke, seid'ne Strümpfe.

BLACK dress-coats and silken stockings,
  Snowy ruffles frilled with art,
Gentle speeches and embraces:—
  Oh, if they but held a heart,—

Held a heart within their bosom,
  Warmed by love which truly glows!
Ah,—I'm wearied with their chanting
  Of imagined lovers' woes!

I will climb upon the mountains,
  Where the quiet cabin stands,
Where the wind blows freely o'er us,
  Where the heart at ease expands.

I will climb upon the mountains,
  Where the dark-green fir-trees grow,
Brooks are rustling, birds are singing,
  And the wild clouds headlong go.

Then farewell, ye polished ladies,
  Polished men, and polished hall!
I will climb upon the mountains,
  Smiling down upon you all.

MOUNTAIN IDYLS.

1.

Auf dem Berge steht die Hütte.

ON yon rock the hut is standing
  Of the ancient mountaineer:
There the dark-green fir-trees rustle,
  And the moon is shining clear.

In that hut there stands an arm-chair,
  Which quaint carvings beautify:
He who sits therein is happy,
  And that happy man am I.

On the stool a girl is sitting,
  On my lap her arms repose,—
With her eyes like blue stars beaming,
  And her mouth a new-born rose.

And the dear blue stars shine on me;
  Full as heaven is their gaze;
And her little lily finger
  Archly on the rose she lays.

"Nay, your mother cannot see us,
  For she spins the whole day long;
And your father plays the cithern
  As he sings a good old song."

And the girl so softly whispers,
  So that none around may hear,—
Many a solemn little secret
  Has she murmured in my ear,—

"Since I lost my aunt, who loved me,
  Now we never more repair
To the shooting-ground at Goslar;
  And it is *so* pleasant there!

"And up here it is so lonely
  On the rocks where cold winds blow;
And in winter we are ever
  Deeply buried in the snow.

"And I'm such a timid creature,
  And I'm frightened like a child
At the evil mountain-spirits
  Who by night are raging wild."

At the thought the maid was silent,
  As if terror thrilled her breast;
And the small hands, white and dimpled,
  To her sweet blue eyes she pressed.

Loud without the fir-trees rustle,
  Loud the spinning-wheel still rings;
And the cithern sounds above them,
  While the father softly sings,

"Dearest child, no evil spirits
  Should have power to cause you dread;
For good angels still are watching
  Night and day around your head."

2.

Tannenbaum mit grünen Fingern.

FIR-TREE with his dark-green fingers
  Taps upon the window low;
And the moon, a yellow listener,
  Casts within her sweetest glow.

Father, mother, both are sleeping,
  Near at hand their rest they take;
But we two, in pleasant gossip,
  Keep each other long awake.

"That you pray, and much too often,
  Seems unlikely, I declare:
On your lips there's a contraction
  Which was never born of prayer.

"Ah, that heartless, cold expression
  Terrifies me as I gaze;
Though a solemn sorrow darkens
  In your eyes their gentle rays.

"And I doubt if you believe in
What is held for truth by most:
Have you faith in God the Father,
In the Son and Holy Ghost?"

"Ah, my darling, when an infant
By my mother's knee I stood,
I believed in God the Father,
He who rules us, great and good;

"He who made the world so lovely,
Gave man beauty, gave him force,
And to sun and moon and planets
Preappointed each their course.

"As I older grew, my darling,
And my way in wisdom won,
I in reason comprehended
And believe now in the Son,—

"In the well-loved Son, who, loving,
Oped the gates of Love so wide,
And for thanks—as is the custom—
By the world was crucified.

"Now, at man's estate arriving,
Full experience I boast,
And, with heart expanded, truly
I believe in the Holy Ghost,

"Who has worked the greatest wonders:
Greater still he'll work again:
He has broken tyrants' strong-holds,
And he breaks the vassal's chain.

"Ancient deadly wounds still healing,
He renews man's ancient right:
All to him, born free and equal,
Are as nobles in his sight.

"Clouds of evil flee before him,
And those cobwebs of the brain
Which forbade us love and pleasure,
Scowling grimly on our pain.

"And a thousand knights well weaponed
Has he chosen, and required
To fulfil his holy bidding,
All with noblest zeal inspired.

"Lo! their precious swords are gleaming,
And their banners wave in fight!
What! you fain would see, my darling,
Such a proud and noble knight?

"Well, then, gaze upon me, dearest;
I am of that lordly host.
Kiss me! I am an elected
True knight of the Holy Ghost!"

3.

Still verdeckt der Mond sich draußen.

SILENTLY the moon goes hiding
Down behind the dark-green trees;
And the lamp which lights our chamber
Flickers in the evening breeze.

But the star-blue eyes are beaming
  Softly o'er the dimpled cheeks,
And the purple rose is gleaming,
  While the gentle maiden speaks:

"Little people—fairy goblins—
  Steal away our meat and bread:
In the chest it lies at evening,
  In the morning it has fled.

"From our milk the little people
  Steal the cream and all the best;
Then they leave the dish uncovered,
  And our cat drinks up the rest.

"And the cat's a witch, I'm certain;
  For by night, when storms arise,
Oft she glides to yonder 'Ghost-Rock,'
  Where the fallen tower lies.

"There was once a splendid castle,
  Home of joy and weapons bright,
Where there swept, in stately torch-dance,
  Lady, page, and armèd knight.

"But a sorceress charmed the castle,
  With its lords and ladies fair.
Now it is a lonely ruin,
  And the owls are nestling there.

"But my aunt has often told me,
  Could I speak the proper word,
In the proper place up yonder,
  When the proper hour occurred,

"Then the walls would change by magic
  To a castle gleaming bright,
And I'd see, in stately dances,
  Dame and page and gallant knight.

"He who speaks the word of power
  Wins the castle for his own,
And the knights, with drum and trumpet,
  Loud will hail him lord alone."

Thus sweet legendary pictures
  From the little rose-mouth bloom;
And the gentle eyes are shedding
  Star-blue lustre through the gloom.

Round my hand the little maiden
  Winds her gold locks as she will,
Gives a name to every finger,
  Kisses, smiles, and then is still.

All things in the silent chamber
  Seem at once familiar grown,
As if e'en the chairs and clothes-press
  Well of old to me were known.

Now the clock talks kindly, gravely,
  And the cithern, as 'twould seem,
Of itself is faintly chiming,
  And I sit as in a dream.

"Now the proper hour is o'er us;
  Here's the place where 't should be heard:
Child, how you would be astonished
  Should I speak the magic word!

"If I spoke that word, then fading
Night would thrill in fearful strife,
Brooks and streams would roar together,
As the castle woke to life.

"Ringing lutes and goblin ditties
From the rifted rock would sound;
Like a mad and merry spring-tide
Flowers grow forest-high around.

"Flowers,—startling, wondrous flowers,
Leaves of vast and fabled form,
Strangely perfumed,—wildly quivering,
As if thrilled with passion's storm.

"Roses, wild as crimson flashes,
O'er the busy tumult rise;
Giant lilies, white as crystal,
Shoot like columns to the skies.

"Great as suns the stars above us
Gaze adown with burning glow;
In the lilies' giant calyx
All their floods of flashes flow.

"We ourselves, my little maiden,
Would be changéd more than all:
Torch-light gleams, o'er gold and satin,
Round us merrily would fall.

"You yourself would be the princess,
And this hut your castle high;
Ladies, lords, and graceful pages
Would be dancing, singing by.

"I, however, I have conquered
 You, and all things, with the word:—
Serfs and castle,—lo! with trumpet,
 Loud they hail me as their lord!"

THE SHEPHERD-BOY.

König ist der Hirtenknabe.

EVERY shepherd is a monarch,
 And a hillock is his throne;
While the sun above him shining
 Is his heavy golden crown.

Sheep before his feet are lying,
 Softest flatterers, crossed with red;
And the calves are "cavalieros,"
 Round they strut with haughty head.

True court-players are the he-goats;
 And the wild-bird and the cow,
With their piping and their herd-bell,
 Are the king's musicians now.

Ever ringing, singing sweetly,
 And as sweetly chime around,
Waterfall and stately fir-trees,
 While the monarch slumbers sound.

And, as he sleeps, his trusty sheep-dog
 As prime minister must reign:
How his snarling and his barking
 Echo over hill and plain!

Dozing, still the monarch murmurs,
"Sure such work was never seen
As this reigning: I were happier
Snug at home beside my queen!

"There my royal head, when weary,
In my queen's arms softly lies,
And my endless, broad dominion,
In her deep and gentle eyes."

THE BROCKEN.

Heller wird es schon im Osten.

IN the East 'tis ever brighter,
Though the sun is dimly gleaming:
Far and wide the mountain-summits
In the misty sea are swimming.

Had I seven-mile boots for travel,
With the wind in wild haste vying,
Over yonder mountain-summits
To *her* house would I go flying.

From the bed where she is sleeping
I would draw the curtain lightly,
Softly kiss her on the forehead,—
On the ruby lips as slightly.

Yet more lightly I would whisper
In the small white ear before me,
"Think in dreams that we ne'er parted,
And that love is ever o'er me."

PRINCESS ILSE.

Ich bin die Prinzessin Ilse.

I AM the Princess Ilse,
And dwell in Ilsenstein:
Come with me to my castle;
Thou shalt be blest,—and mine!

With ever-flowing fountains
I'll cool thy weary brow:
Thou'lt lose, amid the rippling,
The cares which grieve thee now.

In my white arms reposing,
And on my snow-white breast,
Thoul't dream of old, old legends,
And sink in joy to rest.

I'll kiss thee and caress thee,
As in the ancient day
I kissed the Emperor Henry,
Who long has passed away.

The dead are dead and silent:
Only the living love;
And I am fair and blooming,
—Dost feel my wild heart move?

And as my heart is beating,
My crystal castle rings,
Where many a knight and lady
In merry measure springs.

Silk trains are softly rustling,
  Spurs ring from night to morn;
And dwarfs are gayly drumming,
  And blow the golden horn.

As round the Emperor Henry,
  My arms round thee shall fall:
I held his ears,—he heard not
  The trumpet's warning call.

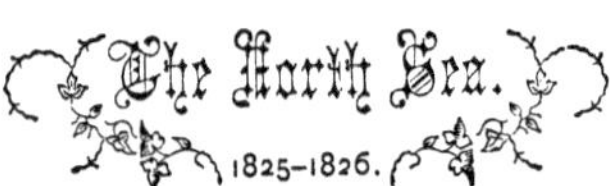

MOTTO: Xenophon's Anabasis, IV. 7.

PART FIRST.

(1825.)

1.

HOMAGE.

Ihr Lieder! Ihr meine guten Lieder!

YE poems! ye mine own valiant poems!
Up, up, and weapon ye!
Let the loud trump be ringing,
And lift upon my shield
The fair young maiden
Who now my heart in full
Shall govern as a sovereign queen.

All hail to thee, thou fair young queen!

From the sun above me
I tear the flashing, ruddy gold,
And weave therefrom a diadem
For thy all-holy head.
From the fluttering, blue-silken heaven's curtain,
Wherein night's bright diamonds glitter,
I cut a costly piece,
To hang as coronation-mantle
Upon thy white, imperial shoulders.
I give to thee, dearest, a city
Of stiffly adorned sonnets,
Proud triple verses, and courteous stanzas;
My wit thy courier shall be,
And for court-fool my fantasy,
As herald, the soft smiling tears in my escutcheon,
And with them my humor.
But I myself, O gentle queen,
I bow before thee, lowly,
And, kneeling on scarlet velvet cushions,
I here offer to thee
The fragments of reason
Which from sheer pity once were left to me
By her who ruled before thee in the realm.

2.

TWILIGHT.

Am blassen Meeresstrande.

ON the white strand of Ocean
Sat I, sore troubled in spirit, and lonely.
The sun sank lower and lower, and cast
Red glowing shadows on the water,
And the snow-white streaming billows,
By the flood impelled,
Foamed up while roaring nearer and nearer,
A wondrous tumult, a whistling and whispering,
A laughing and murmuring, sighing and washing,
And mid them a lullaby known to me only.—
It seemed that I thought upon legends forgotten,
World-old and beautiful stories,
Which I once, when little,
From the neighbors' children had heard,
When we, of summer evenings,
Sat on the steps before the house-door,
Bending us down to the quiet narrative,
With little hearts, a-listening,
And curious, cunning glances,
While near, the elder maidens,
Close by sweet-smelling pots of roses,
At the windows were calmly leaning,
Rosy-hued faces,
Smiling, and lit by the moon.

3.

SUNSET.

Die glühend rothe Sonne steigt.

THE sun in crimsoned glory falls
Down to the broad up-quivering
Gray and silvery ocean-world;
Airy figures, warm in rosy light,
Wave-like roll after; while eastward rising,
From autumn-like darkening veils of vapor,
With sorrowful death-pale features,
Breaks the silent moon.
Like sparks of light behind her,
Cloud-distant, glimmer the planets.

Once there shone in Heaven,
Nobly united,
LUNA the goddess, and SOL the god,
And the bright thronging stars in light swam
round them,
Their little and innocent children.

But evil tongues came whispering quarrels,
And they parted in anger,
The mighty, light-giving spouses.

Now, in the daytime, in loneliest light
The sun-god walks yonder in glory,
All for his lordliness
Ever prayed to and sung by many,
By haughty, heartless, prosperous mortals;

But still by night
In heaven wanders Luna,
The wretched mother,
With all her orphaned starry children;
And she shines in silent sorrow,
And soft-loving maidens and gentle poets
Offer her songs and their sorrows.

The tender Luna! woman at heart,
Loving as ever her beautiful lord,
And at evening, trembling and pale,
Out she peeps from light cloud-curtains,
And looks to the lost one in sorrow.
Fain would she cry, in her anguish, "Come!
Come! the children are longing for love!"
In vain!—the haughty-souled god of fire
Flashes forth at the sight of pale Luna
In doubly deep purple,
For rage and pain,
And all unyielding he hastens down
To his ocean-chilled and lonely bed.

* * * * *

Spirits whispering evil
By their power brought pain and destruction
Even to great gods eternal.
And the poor deities, high in the heavens,
Travel in sorrow,—
Endless, disconsolate journeys;
And they are immortal,
Still bearing with them
Their bright desolation.

But I, the mortal,
Planted so lowly, with death to bless me,
I sorrow no longer.

4.

NIGHT ON THE SEA-SHORE.

Sternlos und kalt ist die Nacht.

STARLESS and cold is the night;
  The wild sea foams;
And over the sea, flat on his face,
  Lies the monstrous, terrible North Wind,
Sighing and sinking his voice as in secret,
Like an old grumbler for once in good humor.
  Unto the ocean he talks,
And he tells her wonderful stories,—
  Giant legends, murderous-humored,
  Very old Sagas of Norway,
And midst them, far sounding, he howls while laughing
  Sorcery-songs from the Edda,
    Gray old Runic sayings,
  So darkly-daring and magical-mighty,
That the snow-white sea-children
High are springing and shouting,
  Drunk with wanton joy.

Meanwhile, on the level, white sea-beach,
Over the sand ever washed by the flood,
Wanders a stranger with wild storming spirit,
And fiercer far than wind and billow.

Go where he may,
Sparks are flashing and sea-shells are cracking,
And he wraps him well in his iron-gray mantle,
And quickly treads through the dark-waving Night,
Safely led by a distant taper
Which, guiding and gladdening, glimmers
From the fisherman's lonely hovel.

Father and brother are on the sea,
And all alone and sad there sits
In the hovel the fisher's daughter,—
The wondrous lovely fisher's daughter.
By the hearth sits she,
Listening to the boiling kettle's
Sweet prophetic, domestic humming,
Scattering light-crackling wood on the fire,
And blows on it,
Till the flashing, ruddy flame-rays
Shine again in magic lustre
On her beautiful features,
On her tender, snow-white shoulder,
Which, moving, comes peeping
Over heavy, dark-gray linen,
And on the little, industrious hand,
Which more firmly binds her under-garment
Round her well-formed figure.
But lo! at once the door springs wide,
And there enters in haste the benighted stranger;
Love-assuring rest his glances
On the foam-white slender maiden,
Who trembling near him stands,

Like a storm-terrified lily;
And he casts on the floor his mantle,
And laughs, and speaks:

"Seest now, my child, I keep my word;
For I am come, and with me comes
The olden time, when the bright gods of heaven
Came once more to the daughters of mortals,
And the daughters of mortals embraced them,
And from them gave birth to
Sceptre-carrying races of monarchs,
And heroes astounding the world.
Yet stare not, my child, any longer
At my divinity,
And, I entreat you, make some tea with rum,
For without, it is cold,
And by such a night air
We too oft freeze,—yes, we, the undying,—
And easily catch the divinest catarrhs
And coughs, which may last us forever."

5.

POSEIDON.

Die Sonnenlichter spielten.

THE sun's bright rays were playing
Over the far-away-rolling sea;
Out in the harbor glittered the ship
Which to my home ere long should bear me;
But we wanted favorable breezes,

And I still sat calm on the snow-white sea-beach,
Alone on the strand,
And I read the song of Odysseus,
The ancient, ever new-born song;
And from its ocean-rippled pages
Joyfully there rose to me
The breath of immortals,
And the light-giving human spring-tide,
And the soft blooming heaven of Hellas.

My noble heart accompanied truly
The son of Laertes in wandering and sorrow,
Set itself with him, troubled in spirit,
By bright-gleaming firesides,
By fair queens, winning, purple-spinning,
And helped him to lie and escape, glad singing,
From giant caverns and nymphs seducing,
Followed behind in fear-boding night,
And in storm and shipwreck,
And thus suffered with him unspeakable sorrow.

Sighing I spoke: "Thou evil Poseidon,
Thy wrath is fearful,
And I myself dread
For my own voyage homeward."

The words were scarce spoken
When up foamed the sea,
And from the snow-white waves arose
The mighty bulrush-crowned sea-god,
And scornful he cried:

"Be not afraid, small poet!
I will not in the least endanger
Thy wretched vessel,
Nor put thy precious being in terror
With all too significant shaking.'
For thou, small poet, hast troubled me not;
Thou hast no turret—though trifling—destroyed
In the great sacred palace of Priam,
Nor one little eyelash hast thou e'er singed
In the eye of my son Polyphemus;
Thee with her counsels did never protect
The goddess of wisdom, Pallas Athené."
And so spake Poseidon,
And sank him again in the sea;
And over the vulgar sailor-joke
There laughed under the water
Amphitrite, the fat old fish-wife,
And the stupid daughters of Nereus.

6.

DECLARATION.

Herangedämmert kam der Abend.

ONWARD dimly came the evening,
Wilder tumbled the waves,
And I sat on the strand, beholding
The swan-like dance of the billows;
And then my breast swelled up like the sea,
And, longing, there seized me a deep home-sickness
For thee, thou lovely form,

Who everywhere art by me,
And everywhere dost call,
Everywhere, everywhere,
In the rustling of breezes, the roaring of Ocean,
And in the sighing of this my sad heart.

With a light reed I wrote in the sand:
"Agnes, I love but thee!"
But wicked waves came washing fast
Over the tender confession,
And wore it away.

Thou too fragile reed, thou false shifting sand,
Ye swift-flowing waters, I trust ye no more!
The heaven grows darker, my heart grows wilder,
And, with strong right hand, from Norway's
forests
I'll tear the highest fir-tree,
And dip it adown
Into Ætna's hot glowing gulf, and with such a
Fiery, flaming, giant graver
I'll inscribe on heaven's jet-black cover,
"Agnes, I love but thee!"

And every night I'll witness, blazing
Above me, the endless flaming verse,
And even the latest races born from me
Will read, exulting, the heavenly motto:
"Agnes, I love but thee!"

7.

BY NIGHT IN THE CABIN.

Das Meer hat seine Perlen.

THE sea has many pearl-drops,
The heaven has many planets,
But this fond heart, my heart,
My heart has tender true love.

Great is the sea and the heaven,
Yet greater is my heart;
And fairer than pearl-drops or planets
Flashes the love in my bosom.

My little gentle maiden,
Come to my beating heart;
My heart, and the sea, and the heaven,
Are lost in loving frenzy.

* * * * *

On the dark-blue heaven-curtain,
Where the lovely stars are gleaming,
Fain would I my lips be pressing,
Press them wildly, storm-like weeping.

And those planets are her bright eyes
But a thousand times repeated;
And they shine and greet me kindly
From the dark-blue heaven-curtain.

To the dark-blue heavenly curtain,
To the eyes I love so dearly,
High my hands I raise devoutly,
And I pray, and I entreat her:

"Lovely eyes, ye lights of mercy,
Oh, I pray ye, bless my spirit;
Let me perish, and exalt me
Up to ye, and to your heaven."

* * * * *

From the heavenly eyes above me
Snow-like sparks are trembling, falling
Through the night, and all my spirit
Wide in love flows forth and wider.

Oh, ye heavenly eyes above me!
Weep your tears upon my spirit,
That those living tears of starlight
O'er my soul may gently ripple.

* * * * *

Cradled calm by waves of ocean,
And by wondrous dreaming, musing
Still I lie within the cabin,
In my gloomy corner hammock,

Through the open hatchway gazing
Yonder to the gleaming starlight,
To the dearest, sweetest glances
Of my sweetest, much-loved maiden.

Yes, those sweetest, best-loved glances
Calm above my head are shining;
They are ringing, they are peeping,
From the dark-blue vault of heaven.

To the dark-blue vault of heaven
Many an hour I gaze in rapture,

Till a snow-white cloudy curtain
Hides from me the best-loved glances.

On the planking of the vessel,
Where my light dreaming head lies,
Leap up the waters,—the wild, dark waters.
They ripple and murmur
Right straight in my ear:

"Thou crazy companion!
Thy arm is short, and the heaven is far,
And the stars up yonder are nailed down firmly;
In vain is thy longing, in vain is thy sighing:
The best thou canst do is to go to sleep."

* * * * *

And I was dreaming of a heath so dreary,
Forever mantled with the sad, white snow,
And 'neath the sad white snow I lay deep buried,
And slept the lonely ice-cold sleep of death.

And yet on high from the dark heaven were
gazing
Adown upon my grave the starlight glances,
Those sad, sweet glances! and they gleamed victorious,
So calmly cheerful, and yet full of true love.

8.

STORM.

Es wüthet der Sturm.

LOUD rages the storm,
And he whips the waves,
And the waters, rage-foaming and rearing,
Tower on high, and with life there come rolling
The snow-white water-mountains,
And the vessel ascends them,
Earnest striving,
Then quickly it darts adown,
In jet-black, wide opening, watery abysses.

O Sea!
Mother of Beauty, born of the foam-billow!
Great Mother of *all* Love! be propitious!
There flutters, corpse-foreboding,
Around us the spectre-like sea-gull,
And whets his sharp bill on the topmast,
And yearns with hunger-lust for the heart
Of him who sounded the praise of thy daughter,
And which thy grandson, the little rogue,
Chose for a plaything.

In vain my entreaties and tears!
My plainings are lost in the terrible storm,
Mid war-cries of north winds;
There's a roaring and whistling, a crackling and howling,
Like a mad-house of noises!
And amid them I hear distinctly

Sweet enticing harp-tones,
Melody mad with desire,
Spirit-melting and spirit-rending;
Well I remember the voices.

Far on the rocky coast of Scotland,
Where the old gray castle towers
Over the wild breaking sea,
In a lofty archéd window
There stands a lovely sickly dame,
Softly transparent and marble pale,
And she plays on the harp and sings;
And through her long locks the wind is waving,
And bears her gloomy song
Over the broad, white, storm-rolling sea.

9.

CALM AT SEA.

Meeresstille! Ihre Strahlen.

OCEAN silence! rays are falling
From the sun upon the water;
Like a train of quivering jewels,
Sweeps the ship's green wake behind us.

Near the rudder lies our boatswain,
On his face, and deeply snoring;
By the mast, his canvas sewing,
Sits a little tarry sailor.

But o'er all his dirty features
Glows a blush, and fear is twitching

Round his full-sized-mouth, and sadly
Gaze his large and glittering eyeballs.

For the captain stands before him,
Fumes and swears, and curses, "Rascal!
Rascal!—there's another herring
Which you've stolen from the barrel!"

Ocean silence! From the water
Up a little fish comes shooting,
Warms its head in pleasant sunlight,
With its small tail merry paddling.

But the sea-gull, sailing o'er us,
Darts him headlong on the swimmer,
And, with claws around his booty,
Flies and fades far, far above me.

10.

A SEA-PHANTOM.

Ich aber lag am Rande des Schiffes.

BUT *I still leaned o'er the side of the vessel,*
Gazing with sad-dreaming glances
Down at the water, clear as a mirror,
Looking yet deeper and deeper,—
Till, deep in the sea's abysses,
At first like dim wavering vapors,
Then slowly,—slowly,—deeper in color,
Domes of churches and towers seemed rising,
And then, as clear as day, a city grand,
Quaint, old-fashioned, Netherlandish,

And living with men,—
Men of high standing, wrapped in black mantles,
With snow-white neck-ruffs, and chains of honor,
And good long rapiers, and good long faces,
Treading in state o'er the crowded market,
To the high steps of the town-hall,
Where stone-carved statues of Kaisers
Kept watch with their swords and sceptres.
Nor distant, near houses in long array,
With windows clear as mirrors,
Stand lindens, cut in pyramidal figures;
And maidens in silk-rustling garments wander,
A golden zone round the slender waist,
With flower-like faces modestly curtained
In jet-black velvet coverings,
From which a ringlet-fulness comes pressing.
Quaint cavalieros in old Spanish dress
Sweep proudly along and salute them.
Elderly ladies,
In dark-brown and old-fashioned garments,
With prayer-book and rosary held in their hands,
Hasten with tripping steps
To the great cathedral,
Attracted by bells' loud ringing
And roaring organ-tones.

E'en I am seized at that far sound
With strange, mysterious trembling.
Infinite longing, wondrous sorrow,
Steal through my heart,—
My heart as yet scarce healed;
It seems as though its wounds, forgotten,

By loving lips again were kissed,
And once again were bleeding
Drops of burning crimson,
Which long and slowly trickle down
Upon an ancient house below there
In the deep, deep sea-town,
On an ancient, high-roofed, curious house,
Where, lone and melancholy,
Below by the window a maiden sits,
Her head on her arm reclined,—
Like a poor and uncared-for child;
And I know thee, thou poor and long-sorrowing
child!

Thou didst hide thus, my dear,
So deep, so deep from me,
In infant-like humor,
And couldst not come up again,
And sattest, strange amid stranger people,
For full five hundred years;
And I meanwhile, my spirit all grief,
Over the whole broad world have sought thee,
And ever have sought thee,
Thou dearly beloved,
Thou long, long lost one,
Thou finally found one,—
At last I have found thee, and now am gazing
Upon thy sweet face,
With earnest, faithful glances,
Still sweetly smiling;
And never will I again on earth leave thee.
I am coming adown to thee,

And with longing, wide-reaching embraces,
Love, I leap down to thy heart!

But just at the right instant
The captain caught and held me safe,
And drew me from danger,
And cried, half-angrily laughing,
"Doctor, is Satan in you?"

11.

PURIFICATION.

Bleib' Du in Deiner Meerestiefe.

STAY thou in gloomy ocean-caverns,
Maddest of dreams,
Thou who hast so many a night
My heart with treacherous joy tormented,
And now, as ocean sprite,
Even by sun-bright day dost annoy me.
Rest where thou art, to eternity,
And I'll cast to thee as offering down
All my long-worn sins and my sorrows,
And the cap and bells of my folly,
Which so long on my head have been ringing,
And the ice-cold glistening serpent-skin
Of hypocrisy
Which so long round my soul has been twining,
The sad, sick spirit,
The God-disbelieving and angel-denying,
Miserable spirit——
Hillo ho! hallo ho! There comes the wind!

Up with the sails! they flutter and belly;
Over the silent, treacherous surface
Hastens the ship,
And loud laughs the spirit set free.

12.

PEACE.

Hoch am Himmel stand die Sonne.

HIGH in heaven the sun was standing,
By cold-white vapors bedimmed.
The sea was still,
And, musing, I lay by the helm of the vessel,
Dreamily musing,—and, half in waking
And half in slumber, I saw in vision
The Saviour of Earth.
In flowing, snow-white garments
He wandered giant-high
Over land and sea;
He lifted his head unto heaven,
His hands were stretched forth in blessing
Over land and sea;
And as a heart in his breast
He bore the sun-orb,
The ruddy, radiant sun-orb,
And the ruddy, radiant, burning heart
Poured forth its beams of mercy
And its gracious and love-blessèd light,
Enlightening and warming,
Over land and sea.

Sweetest bell-tones drew us gayly
Here and there, like swans soft leading
By bands of roses the smooth-gliding ship,
And swam with it sporting to a verdant sea-shore,
Where men were living in a high-towering
And stately town.

Oh, peaceful wonder! How still the town!
Where the sounds of this world were silent,
Of prattling and sultry employment,
And o'er the clean and echoing highways
Mortals were walking, in pure white garments,
Bearing palm-branches,
And whenever two met together,
They saw each other with ready feeling,
And, thrilling with true love and sweet self-denial,
Each pressed a kiss on the forehead,
And looked up on high
To the sun-heart of the Saviour,
Which, gladly atoning his crimson blood,
Flashed down upon them,
And, trebly blessed, thus they spoke:
"Blessed be Jesus Christ!"

PART SECOND.
(1826.)

1.
SEA-GREETING.

Thalatta! Thalatta!

THALATTA! Thalatta!
 Be thou greeted, thou infinite Sea!
Be thou greeted ten thousand times,
With heart wild exulting,
As once thou wert greeted
By ten thousand Grecian spirits,
Striving with misery, longing for home again,
Great, world-famous Grecian true-hearts.

The wild waves were rolling,
Were rolling and roaring;
The sunlight poured headlong upon them
His flickering rosy radiance;
The frightened, fluttering trains of sea-gulls
Went fluttering up, sharp screaming;
Their horses were stamping, the shields were loud
 ringing,
And far it re-echoed, like victor's shout:
Thalatta! Thalatta!

Greeting to thee, thou infinite Sea!
Like the tongue of my country ripples thy water;
Like dreams of my childhood, I saw the glimmer
On thy wild, wavering, watery realm;
And ancient memories again seemed telling
Of all my pleasant and wonderful playthings,
Of all the bright-colored Christmas-presents,
Of all the branches of crimson coral,
Small gold-fish, pearls and beautiful sea-shells,
Which thou in secret ever keep'st
Down there in thy sky-clear crystal home.
Oh, how have I yearned in desolate exile!
Like to a withered floweret
In a botanist's tin herbarium,
Lay the sad heart in my breast;
Or as if I had sat through the weary winter
Sick in a hospital dark and gloomy,
And now I had suddenly left it,
And all bewildering there beams before me
Spring, green as emerald, waked by the sun-rays,
And white tree-blossoms are rustling around me,
And the young flowerets gaze in my face
With eyes perfuming and colored,
Perfuming and humming, and breathing and smiling;
And in the blue heaven sweet birds are singing,
Thalatta! Thalatta!

Thou brave, retreating heart!
How oft, how bitter oft

The barbarous dames of the North have pressed thee round!
From blue eyes, great and conquering,
They shot their burning arrows;
With artful, polished phrases,
Often they threatened to cleave my bosom;
With arrow-head letters full oft they smote
My poor brain, bewildered and lost.—
All vainly held I my shield against them;
Their arrows hissed, and their blows rang round me,
And by the cold North's barbarous ladies
Then was I driven e'en to the sea.
And, free breathing, I hail thee, O Sea!
Thou dearest, rescuing Sea,
Thalatta! Thalatta!

2.

STORM.

Dumpf liegt auf dem Meer das Gewitter.

DARK broods a storm on the ocean,
And through the deep, black wall of clouds
Gleams the zigzag lightning-flash,
Quickly darting and quick departing.
Like a joke from the head of Kronion,
Over the dreary, wild waving water,
Thunder afar is rolling,
And the snow-white steeds of the waves are springing,
Which Boreas himself did beget
On the beautiful mares of Erichthon;

And ocean-birds in their fright are fluttering,
Like shadowy ghosts o'er the Styx,
Which Charon sent back from his shadowy boat.

Little ship, wretched yet merry,
Which yonder art dancing a terrible dance,
Æolus sends thee the fastest companions.
Wildly they're playing the merriest dances;
The first pipes soft, the next blows loud,
The third growls out a heavy basso;
And the tottering sailor stands by the rudder,
And looks incessantly on the compass,
The quivering soul of the ship,
Lifting his hands in entreaty to Heaven:—
O save me, Castor, giant-like hero,
And thou who fight'st with fist, Polydeuces!

3.

THE SHIPWRECKED.

Hoffnung und Liebe! Alles zertrümmert!

LOST hope and lost love! All is in ruins!
And I myself, like a dead body
Thrown back by the angry sea,
Lie on the sea-beach:
On the waste, barren sea-beach,
Before me rolls a waste of water,
Behind me lies starvation and sorrow,
And above me are rolling the storm-clouds,
The formless, dark-gray daughters of air,
Which from the sea, in cloudy buckets,

Scoop up the water,
Ever wearied lifting and lifting,
And then pour it again in the sea,—
A mournful, wearisome business,
And useless, too, as this life of mine.
The waves are murm'ring, the sea-gulls screaming,
Old remembrances seem floating round,
Long-vanished visions, long-faded pictures,
Torturing, yet sweet, seem living once more!

There lives a maid in Norland,
A lovely maid, right queenly fair;
Her slender, cypress-like figure
Is clasped by a passionate snowy-white robe:
The dusky ringlet-fulness,
Like a night of rapture,
From the lofty braid-crowned forehead comes pouring,
Twining all dreamily sweet
Round the sweet and snow-pale features;
And from the sweet and snow-pale features,
Great and wondrous, gleams a dark eye,
Like a sun of jet-black fire.

O thou bright black sun, how oft,
Enraptured oft, I drank from thee
Wild glances of inspiration,
And stood all quivering, drunk with their fire,—
And then swept a smile all mild and dove-like
Round the lips high mantling, proud and lovely;
And the lips high mantling, proud and lovely,

Breathed forth words as sweet as moonlight,
Soft as the perfume of roses :—
Then my soul rose up in rapture
And flew, like an eagle, high up into heaven!

Hush! ye billows and sea-mews!
All is long over,—hope and fortune,
Fortune and true love! I lie on the sea-beach,
A weary and wreck-ruined man,
Still pressing my face, hot glowing,
Into the cold, wet sand.

4.

SUNSET.

Die schöne Sonne.

THE beautiful sun-orb
Has calmly sunk down to his rest in the sea;
The wild-rolling waters already are dyed
With night's dark shade,
Though still the evening crimson
Strews them with light, as yet bright-golden,
And the stern roaring might of the flood
Crowds to the sea-beach the snowy billows,
All merrily quickly leaping,
Like white woolly flocks of lambkins,
Which youthful shepherds at evening, singing,
Drive to their homes.

"How fair is the sun-orb!"
Thus spoke, his silence breaking, my friend,

Who with me on the sea-beach loitering,
And jesting half, and half in sorrow,
Assured me that the bright sun was
A lovely dame, whom the old ocean-god
For "convenience" once had married.
And in the daytime she wanders gayly
Through the high heaven, purple-arrayed,
And all in diamonds gleaming,
And all beloved and all amazing
To every worldly being,
And every worldly being rejoicing
With warmth and splendor from her glances;
Alas! at evening, sad and unwilling,
Back must she bend her slow steps
To the dripping home, to the barren embrace,
Of grisly old age.

"Believe me,"—added to this my friend,
And smiling and sighing, and smiling again,—
"They're leading below there the lovingest life!
For either they're sleeping or they are scolding,
Till high uproars above here the sea,
And the fisher in watery roar can hear
How the Old One his wife abuses:—
'Plump drab of the universe!
Wooing with radiance!
All the long day you are burning for other loves,
By night, to me, you are freezing and weary.'
After such a curtain-lecture,
Of course the Sun-bride falls to weeping,
Falls to weeping, and wails her sorrow,
And cries so wretchedly, that the Sea-god

Quickly, all desperate, leaps from his bed,
And straight to the ocean-surface comes rising,
To get to fresh air,—and his senses.

"So I beheld him, but yesterday night,
Rising breast-high from the ocean.
He wore a long jacket of yellow flannel,
And a new night-cap, white as a lily,
And a wrinkled, faded old face."

5.

THE SONG OF THE OCEANIDES.

Abendlich blasser wird es am Meer.

COLDER the twilight falls on the Ocean,
And lonely, with his own lonelier spirit,
There sits a man on the barren strand,
And casts death-chilling glances on high,
To the wide-spread, death-chilling vault of heaven,
And looks on the broad, wide wavering sea;
And over the broad, wide wavering sea,
Like air-borne sailors, his sighs go sweeping,
Returning once more in sadness,
But to discover, firm fastened, the heart
Wherein they fain would anchor;—
And he groans so loud that the snow-white sea-mews,
Frightened up from their nests in the sand-heaps,
Around in white clouds flutter,
And he speaks unto them the while, and laughing:

"Ye black-legged sea-fowl,
With your white pinions o'er the sea fluttering,

With crooked dark bills drinking the sea-water,
And rank, oily seal-blubber devouring,
Your wild life is bitter, e'en as your food is!
While I here, the fortunate, taste only sweet things!
I taste the sweetest breath of roses,
The nourished-with-moonshine nightingale bride;
I eat the most delicate sugar *méringues*,
And the sweetest of all I've tasted,—
Sweetest true love, and sweetest returned love.

"She loves me! she loves me! the lovely maiden!
She now stands at home,—perhaps at the window,
And looks through the twilight, afar on the highway,
And looks and longs but for me,—now, really!
All vainly she gazes around, still sighing,
Then, sighing, she walks adown in the garden,
Wandering in moonlight and perfume,
And speaks to the sweet flowers,—often telling them
How I, the beloved one, deserve her love,
And am *so* agreeable,—that's certain!
In bed reposing, in slumber, in dreams,
There flits round her, happy, my well-loved form;
E'en in the morning at breakfast,
On the glittering bread and butter
She sees my dear features sweet smiling,
And she eats it up out of love:—that's certain!"

Thus he's boasting and boasting,
And mid it all sounds the scream of the sea-gulls,
Like old and ironical tittering;
The evening vapors are climbing up;
From clouds of violet, strange and dream-like,

Out there peeps the grass-yellow moon;
High are roaring the ocean billows,
And deep from the high up-roaring sea,
All sadly as whispering breezes,
Sounds the lay of the Oceanides,
The beautiful, kind-hearted water-fairies;
And clearest among them the sweet notes are ringing
Of the silver-footed bride of Peleus,
And they sigh, and are singing:

"O fool, thou fool! thou weak, boasting fool!
Thou tortured with sorrows!
Vanished and lost are the hopes thou hast cherished,
The light sporting babes of thy heart's love;
And ah! thy heart, thy Niobe heart
By grief turned to stone!
And in thy wild brain 'tis night,
And through it is darting the lightning of madness;
And thou boastest from anguish!
O fool! thou fool, thou weak, boasting fool!
Stiff-necked art thou, like thy first parent,
The noblest of Titans, who from the immortals
Stole heavenly fire and on Man bestowed it,
And, eagle-tortured, to rocks firm fettered,
Defied Olympus, enduring and groaning,
Until we heard it deep down in the sea,
And gathered around him with songs consoling.

"O fool, thou fool! thou weak, boasting fool!
Thou who art weaker by far than he,
Hadst thou thy reason thou'dst honor th' immortals,
And bear with more patience the burden of suffering,

And bear it in patience, in silence, in sorrow,
Till even Atlas his patience had lost,
And the heavy world from his shoulders was thrown
Into endless night."

So rang the deep song of the Oceanides,
The lovely compassionate water-spirits,
Until the wild waters had drowned their music.
Behind the dark clouds down sank the moon,
Tired Night was yawning,
And I sat yet a while in darkness, sad weeping.

6.

THE GODS OF GREECE.

Vollblühender Mond! In deinem Licht.

THOU full-blooming moon! In thy soft light,
Like wavering gold, bright shines the sea;
Like morn's first radiance, yet dimly enchanted,
It lies o'er the broad, wide, strand's horizon;
And in the pure blue starless heaven
The snowy clouds are sweeping,
Like giant-towering shapes of immortals
Of white gleaming marble.

Nay, but I err; no clouds are those yonder!
Those are in person the great gods of Hellas,
Who once so joyously governed the world,
But now, long banished, long perished,
As monstrous, terrible spectres are sweeping
Along o'er the midnight heaven.

Gazing and strangely bewildered, I see
The airy Pantheon,
The awfully silent, fearfully sweeping,
Giant-like spectres.

He there is Kronion, the King of Heaven.
Snow-white are the locks of his head,
The far-famed locks which send throbs through
Olympus.
He holds in his hand the extinguished bolt,
Sorrow and suffering sit stern on his brow,
Yet still it hath ever its ancient pride.
Once there were lorldlier ages, O Zeus,
When thou didst revel divinely,
On youths and maidens and hecatombs many!
But e'en the immortals may not reign forever;
The younger still banish the elder,
As thou thyself didst thy gray old father,
And drove from their kingdom thy Titan uncles,
Jupiter Parricida!
Thee too I know well, haughty Juno!
Spite of all thy fearful jealousy,
Though from thee another thy sceptre hath taken
And thou art no more the Queen of heaven,
And thy wondrous eyes seem frozen,
And even thy lily-white arms are powerless,
And never more can fall thy vengeance
On the god-impregnated maiden
And the wonder-effecting son of Jove.
Well too I know thee, Pallas Athené!
With shield and wisdom still thou couldst not
Avert the sad fall of immortals!

Thee too I know now,—yes, thee, Aphrodite!
Once the Golden One,—now the Silver One!
E'en yet the charm of thy girdle adorns thee;
But I shudder in secret before thy beauty,
And though I were blessed with thy beautiful body,
Like other heroes, I'd perish with fear;
As the goddess of corpses thou seemest to me,
Venus Libitina!
No more in fond love looks on thee,
There, the terrible Ares;
Sadly is gazing Phœbus Apollo,
The youthful. His lyre sounds no more,
Which once rang with joy at the feasts of the gods.
And sadder still looks Hephaistos,
And—truly the limping one!—nevermore
Will he fill the office of Hebe,
And busily pour out, in the Assembly,
The sweet-tasting nectar.—And long hath been silent
The ne'er-to-be-silenced laugh of immortals.

Gods of old time, I never have loved ye!
For the Greeks did never chime with my spirit,
And even the Romans I hate at heart;
But holy compassion and shuddering pity
Stream through my soul
As I now gaze upon ye, yonder,
Gods long neglected,
Death-like, night-wandering shadows,
Weak and fading, scattered by the wind;
And when I remember how weak and windy
The gods now are who o'er you triumphed,—
The new and the sorrowful gods now ruling,

The joy-destroyers in lamb-robes of meekness,—
Then there comes o'er me gloomiest rage;
Fain would I shatter the modern temples,
And battle for ye, ye ancient immortals,
For ye and your good old ambrosial right,
And before your lofty altars,
Once more erected, with incense sweet smoking,
Would I once more, kneeling, adoring,
Raise up my arms to you in prayer.

For constantly, ye old immortals,
Was it your custom, in mortal battles,
Ever to lend your aid to the conqueror:
Therefore is man now far nobler than you,
And in the contest I now take part
With the cause of the conquered immortals.

* * * * * *

'Twas thus I spoke, and blushes were visible
Over the cold white aerial figures,
Gazing upon me like dying ones
With pain transfigured: they quickly vanished.
The moon concealed her features
Behind a cloud, which darkly came sweeping:
Loudly the sea rose foaming,
And the beautiful calm-beaming stars victorious
Shone out o'er heaven.

7.

QUESTIONING.

Am Meer, am wüsten, nächtlichen Meer.

BY the sea, by the dreary, darkening sea,
Stands a youthful man,

His heart all sorrowing, his head all doubting,
And with gloomy lips he questions the billows:

"Oh, solve me Life's riddle, I pray ye,
The torturing ancient enigma
Over which many a brain hath long puzzled,
Old heads in hieroglyph-marked mitres,
Heads in turbans and caps mediæval,
Wig-covered pates, and a thousand others,
Sweating, wearying heads of mortals:—
Tell me, what meaneth *Man?*
Whence came he hither? Where goes he hence?
Who dwells there on high in the radiant planets?"

The billows are murmuring their murmur unceasing.
Wild blows the wind, the dark clouds are fleeting,
The stars are still gleaming, so calmly and cold,
And a fool waits for an answer.

8.

THE PHŒNIX.

Es kommt ein Vogel geflogen aus Westen.

A BIRD from the far west his way came winging.
Still flying eastward,
To the beautiful land of gardens,
Where sweetest spices are breathing and growing,
And palm-trees rustle, and brooks are rippling;
And, flying, sings the bird so wondrous:

"She loves him! she loves him!
She bears his form in her little bosom,

And wears it sweetly and secretly hidden,
Yet she knows it not yet!
Only in dreams he comes to *her*,
And she prays and weeps, his hand oft kissing,
His name often calling,
And calling she wakens, and lies in terror,
And presses in wonder those eyes soft gleaming:—
She loves him! she loves him!"

9.

ECHO.

An den Mastbaum gelehnt, auf dem hohen Verdeck.

I LEANED on the mast; on the lofty ship's deck
Standing, I heard the sweet song of a bird.
Like steeds of dark green, with their manes of bright silver,
Sprang up the white and wild curling billows.
Like trains of wild swans went sailing past us,
With shimmering canvas, the Helgolanders,
The daring *nomades* of the North Sea.
Over my head, in the infinite blue,
Went sailing a snowy white cloud.
Bright flamed the sun, burning forever,
The rose of heaven, the fire-blossoming,
Who, joyful, mirrored his rays in ocean,
Till heaven and sea, and my heart besides,
Rang back with the echo:
She loves him! she loves him!

10.

IN PORT.

Glücklich der Mann, der den Hafen erreicht hat.

HAPPY the man who is safe in his haven,
And has left far behind the sea and its sorrows,
And now so warm and calmly sits
In the cosy Town-Cellar of Bremen.

Oh, how the world so home-like and sweetly
In the wine-cup again is mirrored,
And how the wavering *microcosmos*
Sunnily flows through the thirstiest heart!
All things I see in the glass,—
Ancient and modern histories by myriads,
Grecian and Ottoman, Hegel and Gans,
Forests of citron, and watches patrolling,
Berlin, and Schilda, and Tunis, and Hamburg,
But above all the form of the loved one,
An angel's head on a Rhine-wine-gold ground.

Oh, how fair! how fair art thou, beloved!
Thou art as fair as roses!
Not like the roses of Shiraz,
The brides of the nightingale, sung by old Hafiz!
Not like the rose of Sharon,
Holily blushing and hallowed by prophets;
Thou art like the rose in the cellar of Bremen!*

---

* In the Rathskeller—Council-Cellar or Town-Hall Cellar—of Bremen, there is kept a celebrated tun, called "THE ROSE," containing wine three hundred years old. Around it are the "TWELVE

That is the Rose of Roses:
The older she grows, the sweeter she blossoms,
And her heavenly perfume has made me happy,
It has inspired me,—has made me tipsy;
And were I not held by the shoulder fast
By the Town-Cellar Master of Bremen,
I had gone rolling over!

The noble soul! we sat there together,
And drank, too, like brothers,
Discoursing of lofty, mysterious matters,
Sighing and sinking in solemn embraces.
He made me a convert to Love's holy doctrine;
I drank to the health of my bitterest enemy,
And I forgave the worst of all poets,
As I myself some day shall be forgiven;
Till, piously weeping, before me
Silently opened the gates of redemption,
Where the twelve Apostles—the holy barrels—
Preach in silence, and yet so distinctly,
Unto all nations.

Those are the fellows!
Invisible outward in sound oaken garments,
Yet they within are more lovely and radiant

APOSTLES," or hogsheads filled with wine of a lesser age. When a bottle is drawn from the Rose, it is supplied from one of the Apostles; and by this arrangement the contents of the Rose are kept up to the requisite standard of antiquity. Those who are familiar with the writings of HAUFF will remember the exquisite and genial sketch entitled "A Fantasy in the Rathskeller of Bremen."—TRANSLATOR.

Than all the proudest priests of the Temple
And the lifeguardsmen and courtiers of Herod,
Glittering in gold and arrayed in rich purple;—
Still I have ever maintained
That not amid common, vulgar people,
No, but in the *élite* of society,
Constantly lived the monarch of heaven.

Hallelujah! How sweetly wave round me
The palm-trees of Bath-El!
How sweet breathe the myrrh-shrubs of Hebron!
How Jordan ripples and tumbles with gladness,
And my own immortal spirit tumbleth,
And I tumble with it, and, tumbling,
I'm helped up the stairway into broad daylight,
By the brave Council-Cellar Master of Bremen!

Thou brave Council-Cellar Master of Bremen!
Seest thou upon the roofs of the houses sitting
The angels?—and they are all tipsy and singing;
The radiant sun, too, yonder in heaven,
Is only a crimson, wine-colored proboscis,
Which the World-Soul protrudeth,
And round the red nose of the World-Soul
Goes whirling the whole of the tipsified world.

11.

EPILOGUE.

Wie auf dem Felde die Waizenhalmen.

AS in the meadow the wheat is growing,
So, sprouting and waving in mortal souls,
Thoughts are growing.
Ay,—but the soft inspirations of poets
Are like the blue and crimson flowerets
Blossoming amid them.
Blue and crimson blossoms,
The ill-natured reaper rejects ye as useless,
Blockheaded simpletons scorn ye while threshing;
Even the penniless wanderer,
Who by your sight is made glad and inspired,
Shakes his head,
And calls ye weeds, though lovely.
Only the fair peasant maiden,
The one who twines her garlands,
Honors you truly, and plucks you,
And decks with you her lovely tresses,
And, when thus adorned, to the dance hastens,
Where the pipe and the viol are merrily pealing;
Or to the tranquil beech-tree,
Where the voice of the loved one more pleasantly sounds
Than the pipe or the viol.